END OF AN ERA

MAD MEN
&
THE ORDEAL OF CIVILITY

by

JAMES J. O'MEARA

Counter-Currents Publishing Ltd.
San Francisco
2015

Cover design by Kevin I. Slaughter

Published in the United States by
COUNTER-CURRENTS PUBLISHING LTD.
P.O. Box 22638
San Francisco, CA 94122
USA
http://www.counter-currents.com/

Hardcover ISBN: 978-1-940933-35-1
Paperback ISBN: 978-1-940933-36-8
E-book ISBN: 978-1-940933-37-5

CONTENTS

Introduction: Mad Mansplaining ❖ iii

1. Mad *Männerbund*? ❖ 1

2. Mad Manspreading? ❖ 8

3. *Mad Men* Jumps the Gefilte Fish, Part 1:
Missed Congeniality ❖ 18

4. *Mad Men* Jumps the Gefilte Fish, Part 2:
The Country of the Blind ❖ 42

5. "This is a Shirtsleeve Operation":
Judaic Crypsis in the Final Season of *Mad Men* ❖ 68

6. Don Draper's Last Diddle:
The Finale of *Mad Men* ❖ 78

Index ❖ 85

About the Author ❖ 98

ARTHUR CASE: You're so profoundly sad.

BETTY DRAPER: No. It's just my people are Nordic.

— *Mad Men*: "The Benefactor" (Episode 2.3, 2008)

Introduction
MAD MANSPLAINING

Mad Men as a television and indeed cultural phenomenon needs, of course, no introduction.

This collection, on the other hand, may need some 'splaining. It brings together essays I've written at various times, all published on the Counter-Currents/ *North American New Right* website, arising out of my own fascination with the show and the phenomenon, from the pilot to the finale.

Over this time, my views on the show, and my angle of approach, have varied. The first essay — "Mad *Männerbund?*" — is written from the same alt-Right "masculinist" perspective that characterized many of my first essays for Counter-Currents, and indeed it appeared in my first collection.[1] Here, I was mining the *Mad Men* phenomenon, with its alternatively nostalgic, ironic, and fetishized view of '60s fashion, for hopeful signs of a Third Way between the drab Right and the sissified Left, as well as suggesting that a return to earlier ideas of masculine attire would actually serve a strategic purpose.

As the series developed, the anti-Aryan bias of the show's creators became distracting, and I began to lose interest. Then, certain plot developments caught my attention, and I began to notice certain archetypal themes emerging. Thus emerged a series of essays — or one big essay — devoted to a close, perhaps paranoiac,[2]

---

[1] James J. O'Meara, *The Homo and the Negro: Masculinist Meditations on Politics and Popular Culture*, ed. Greg Johnson (San Francisco: Counter-Currents, 2012).

[2] "The ability of the brain to perceive links between things

reading of the show as dramatizing, perhaps accidentally, the Judaic "ordeal of civility"[3] — the confrontation with, rather than assimilation to, Aryan civilization.

Feeling an obligation to see the thing through — or thoroughly brainwashed by network propaganda — I made a deliberate effort to watch the last two episodes — the network-promised "end of an era," as if it would be remembered like the moon landing or the JFK assassination — and found the anti-assimilationist, outright triumphalist agenda in full view, resulting in the last two essays here.

And still, *Mad Men*, like Howard Beale, the Mad Prophet of the Airwaves, would not leave me alone. No sooner had the show wrapped than the "man-spreading" kerfuffle arose, requiring me return to Season One for advice. In further defiance of the Judeo-Christian obsession with "progress," this essay, though last in composition, has spiraled around to

---

which rationally are not linked. Dalí described the paranoiac-critical method as a 'spontaneous method of irrational knowledge based on the critical and systematic objectivity of the associations and interpretations of delirious phenomena.' Employing the method when creating a work of art uses an active process of the mind to visualize images in the work and incorporate these into the final product. An example of the resulting work is a double image or multiple image in which an ambiguous image can be interpreted in different ways. André Breton . . . hailed the method, saying that . . . it 'has immediately shown itself capable of being applied equally to painting, poetry, the cinema, the construction of typical Surrealist objects, fashion, sculpture, the history of art, and even, if necessary, all manner of exegesis.'" — Wikipedia, http://en.wikipedia.org/wiki/Paranoiac-critical_method.

[3] John Murray Cuddihy, *The Ordeal of Civility: Freud, Marx, Levi-Strauss, and the Jewish Struggle With Modernity* (New York: Basic Books, 1974).

find its snug home in second place.

I collect them here and offer them as a retrospective or even a memento,[4] as a, frankly, unique perspective on a cultural phenomenon, and as a preview of ideas and angles of approach that you will find more fully developed in such forthcoming collections from Counter-Currents as *Green Nazis in Space: New Essays on Literature, Art, & Culture* and *Passing the Buck: A Traditionalist Goes to the Movies*.

As always, I owe thanks to Dr. Greg Johnson for making all this possible, and to the readers on Counter-Currents, Facebook, and elsewhere online, who offered encouragement and critique.

Rustbelt, USA
June 4, 2015

EPISODES DISCUSSED

S1, Ep1 (19 Jul. 2007) "Smoke Gets in Your Eyes,"
S1, Ep2 (26 Jul. 2007) "Ladies Room,"
S1, Ep12 (11 Oct. 2007) "Nixon vs. Kennedy,"
S2, Ep3 (10 Aug. 2008) "The Benefactor,"
S5, Ep11 (27 May 2012) "The Other Woman,"
S5, Ep12 (3 Jun. 2012) "Commissions and Fees,"
S7, Ep12 (3 May 2015) "Lost Horizon,"
S7, Ep13 (10 May 2015) "The Milk and Honey Route,"
S7, Ep14 (17 May 2015) "Person to Person,"

---

[4] "And nonetheless I still write this gothic love song / A sign to myself / And the memory of my past . . ." — David Tibet, "A Gothic Love Song."

Mad *Männerbund*?

In the first couple chapters of *Men Among the Ruins*, Julius Evola outlines the nature of the State as constituted by Authority from above (as opposed to from below, as in democracy or party dictatorship), as represented by an Order of men, "who differentiate themselves from the masses as the bearers of a complete and legitimate authority," originating in the primitive *Männerbünde*. Thus: "The true task and necessary premise for the rebirth of the 'nation' . . . consists of . . . re-establishing a virile substance in the form of a political elite around which a new crystallization will occur."[1]

One must ask, how would this Order be constituted? For example, would they have snappy uniforms?

This is not a frivolous question. Some kind of unified look seems necessary for the requisite unity of purpose, and simple identification as an Order by the masses. And certainly, uniforms always seem to preoccupy Rightist groups.

But while Hitler's Brown Shirts and black SS were a hit in Germany (due, as Evola would recognize, precisely to the remaining respect for traditional authority that made Central Europe seem recoverable), uniforms are quite problematic in Anglo-American society. Mosley's Black Shirts were easily satirized, while various post-War American "Neo-Nazi" groups are widely ridiculed ("I hate Illinois Nazis!").[2]

---

[1] Julius Evola, *Men Among the Ruins: Post-War Reflections of a Radical Traditionalist*, ed. Michael Moynihan, trans. Guido Stucco (Rochester, Vt.: Inner Traditions, 2002), p. 132.

[2] http://www.youtube.com/watch?v=jhozx819izU

Indeed, in the context of Post War, "casual" America, uniforms are always bad, unless they partake of the democratic slob ethic. Thus, motorcycle gangs can wear ragged remnants of German uniforms, along with their piss-drenched "colors"; Negroes seem to enjoy wearing full camo outfits in urban settings; and the various Guardian Angels, who are also largely figures of fun, dress like guidos in berets, even in Texas.

The mere portrayal of a "uniform" is itself a Bad Thing, sufficient to indicate fear and loathing of the person wearing it.

I believe Mark Ames once suggested a mass protest by people wearing Gap khakis and button-down shirts, during the Republican convention in New York City, to show that Bush's opponents were not just the dirty hippies stewing in the "Free Speech Zones." But really, this is the schlubby non-style of the cubicle rat, not fit for a vanguard movement.

Yet he may have something there.

Ironically, while the hippies officially celebrated the wild, "do your own thing" style of say, dressing like Sgt. Pepper, in practice they quickly devolved into the lazy, dirty, "crunchy" style of the jeans-and-t-shirt identikit, emblematic of the fact that for all their talk of "your own thing" they were actually a movement of fusion into a Dionysian indiscernibility (or "promiscuity" as Evola would say, an interesting term to use in the area of "free love"), exemplified by the "Woodstock Nation," orgies, "mass" protests, etc.

However, maybe the Hippies had the right intuition. What did they sneer at as "uniforms"?

Suits. Men's business suits. And unlike jackbooted Nazis, not only merely acceptable, but even compulsory, at least at one time: the period of America's post-war dominance. And in today's Casual Friday world, the ultimate rebellion.

This is not the place for a history of suits, which you can easily find. I just want to observe here that at one time, suits, though uniforms, could make statements, and even change history. Consider the JFK Look, two buttons, no hat: Youth! Or the Beatles' tight collarless look, itself derived (via the homosexual Brian Epstein) from the Teddy (i.e. Edwardian) Boys of the '50s; and, of course, the Lonely Hearts Club Band uniforms: Rebellion!

Among other things, Kennedy banished hats for men, even disposing of the top hat for his inauguration speech. He also traded in the three-button suit for a baggier two-button style (to accommodate his back brace) and reintroduced the casual blue blazer both in the White House and on trips to Hyannis Port. Less well known is that for all the unselfconscious air that his wardrobe conveyed, JFK went to the trouble of having much of it made by a tailor in London, a sartorial standard he had come to appreciate as the son of US Ambassador Joe Kennedy and one that his wife Jackie and sister-in-law Lee Radziwill thought should be the natural beginning point for a man of style.

In the Beatles' pre-famous days, leather and cowboy boots were the order of the day. (In other words, fake British Cowboy nonsense, like Bush.) When Brian Epstein signed the boys, he changed their image to fit in with their new tight sound. Their hair was cut in a shorter version on the now famous Beatles' mop-top, and their old leathers changed for collarless tailored suits.

When the Beatles entered their Sgt. Pepper stage they were wearing psychedelic flared suits, army style jackets, and identical mustaches. There was a sense of freedom and unrealness about their new image which favored the times.

After they had outgrown that look, they outgrew their hair and beards and became fully fledged hippies. They wore Indian style clothes away on their meditation and relaxation trips, and jeans, shirts, and cowboy garb in their final days. (In other words, after they passed their prime they became dirty hippie slobs.) However, Ringo was notorious in his love for suits.

All this is nicely summarized in the first chapter of Tom Wolfe's *The Electric Kool-Aid Acid Test*, titled "Shiny Black FBI Shoes," where white-suited Wolfe (who informs the reader that in New York he is considered quite stylish) finds himself feeling threatened by Men-in-Black FBI agents, and at the same time feeling out-classed by a Merry Prankster in a colorful and be-medaled WWI era uniform.

Where might we find vestiges of this be-suited rebellion today, to serve as models for our new Order?

I submit, the popular TV show, *Mad Men.*.

Of course, the various Mad Men are not themselves rebels. Quite the contrary, they are deliberately portrayed in their easy, taken-for-granted post-Kennedy, pre-Beatles period of dominance, which is exactly why they can serve as our model for the unselfconscious authority of the New Order.

And yes, "*Mad Men* is an unpleasant little entry in the genre of Now We Know Better," as Mark Greif (!?) says in the *London Review of Books*, but this doesn't prevent us from detourning the show and its images any way we want, just as teens took Dean and Brando as models, not warnings:

Beneath the Now We Know Better is a whiff of

Doesn't That Look Good. The drinking, the cigarettes, the opportunity to slap your children! The actresses are beautiful, the Brilliantine in the men's hair catches the light, and everyone and everything is photographed as if in stills for a fashion spread. The show's "1950s" is a strange period that seems to stretch from the end of World War Two to 1960, the year the action begins. The less you think about the plot the more you are free to luxuriate in the low sofas and Eames chairs, the gunmetal desks and geometric ceiling tiles and shiny IBM typewriters. Not to mention the lush costuming: party dresses, skinny brown ties, angora cardigans, vivid blue suits and ruffled peignoirs, captured in the pure dark hues and wide lighting ranges that Technicolor never committed to film.

Greif even picks up a bit on the *Männerbund* subtext:

The Sopranos, the programme for which *Mad Men*'s creator Matthew Weiner worked as a writer before getting his own series, is often invoked by journalists as a godparent to the newer show. The two share a focus on the world of men, a primary relationship between an older, world-weary boss and a sneaky young turk, even a psychiatrist figure who pops up to allow a character to express what can't be said at home. Unfortunately for *Mad Men*, the example of *The Sopranos* shows up all the possibilities of the medium that aren't exploited in Weiner's show. And unfortunately for Jon Hamm, James Gandolfini's depiction of Tony Soprano shows the kind of man Don Draper might have been:

someone in whom strength and weakness, allure and cruel cunning, were held in balance, through an alternation of authority, neediness, and physical violence.

I suggest that the immense popularity of both *The Sopranos* (what a sissy name!) and *Mad Men* is both a symptom of the vaguely felt need for an elite Order in our society, whether it be found in *Mad Men* or mobsters (snappy dressers, and from Evola's Sicily!), as well as a suggestion for how to begin to proceed to reconstitute one.

Although, sartorially, I certainly hope the *Mad Men* model prevails over the *Goodfellas* look.

The fact that apparently there's a whole bunch of women behind the show trying to bring down patriarchy is itself evidence of the matriarchal/social vs. patriarchal/state dichotomy that Evola is working from.

One aspect of the *Männerbund* is a masculinist homoeroticism if not necessarily homosexuality, and while *The Sopranos* seemed to have a hard time handling that (whacking one outed character and having Tony's son choose a series of queer careers, like event planning and film intern), *Mad Men* has a more interesting texture.

One character is closeted (although we are supposed to congratulate ourselves on seeing how obvious he is), one rather minor one is open and mocked; while last week we find that the odious Pete Campbell is not only a wimpy, weaselly little guy (the "sneaky young turk" of Greif's description) who would be typed as "gay" in our MTV-thug culture, but he also can dance, and you know what that means. (By "can dance" I mean knows how to do some old time White people dance, not the Negroid twitching Evola mocks.)

Additionally, the one female copywriter gets stoned and seems to be coming on to her middle-aged secretary; this might explain why she was attracted to Campbell. Since the first episode has Draper mocking Freud, is it possible that Otto Weininger, if not Hans Blüher, is punching up the scripts?

Counter-Currents/*North American New Right*,
June 3, 2015

MAD MANSPREADING?

"Keep it up, and even if you do get my job you'll never run this place. You'll die in that corner office, a midlevel executive with a little bit of hair who women go home with out of pity. Want to know why? Because no one will like you."

— Don Draper to Pete Campbell[1]

The poohbahs of the manosphere often put me in mind of the Stalinist shop steward played by Peter Sellers in *I'm All Right, Jack*—the response to any situation is always the same: round up the boys, jump on a barrel, and shout "They're doin' it to us again, mates!"

The latest kerfuffle involves something called "manspreading," and the attempts of first London, then New York, to ban same when aboard public transit.

Now, sometimes "conservatives" love banning stuff, at least when the ban inconveniences someone else. Pull up your pants! No skateboarding! No roller skates! Turn off that damn transistor radio![2] No breastfeeding! Put on a blouse, you skank![3]

On other occasions, their own ox is gored, or so they feel, and off they go to defend their inalienable

---

[1] *Mad Men*, Season 1, Episode 1, "Smoke Gets in Your Eyes."

[2] "No more fun of any kind!" — Dean Wormer, *Animal House*. I've previously identified the snobs vs. slobs meme in *Mad Men*, but sometimes, as conservatives like to say, the stereotypes are true.

[3] For some unexplained reason, there are no women among conservatives.

rights to inconvenience everyone else.[4]

This time it's "manspreading," the subway graffiti "art" of the Right. "Hey, the kid's an artist, he dindu nuffin anyways!" And inconvenience is what it's about. As a long-time subway rider, I can assure you it's about accommodating increasingly obese Americans on trains, not another feminazi castration ploy; no different than if Jack Donovan, say, chose to light up a Havana on the L train.[5]

Of course, arrest seems a bit over the top, especially in a city where the new tribal Big Man, Papa Doc De Blasio, has called for the scaling back or elimination of enforcement actions against scores of so-called "quality of life" infractions, such as public urination[6] or even

---

[4] The history of the Right's infatuation with smoking, for example, from Ayn Rand's "sign of the dollar" cigarettes to Wendell Berry's down-home tobacky farming, to now Tito Purdue, whose *Reuben* manages to combine both—his Lee farms the sot-weed, while the titular Reuben exemplifies his *Übermensch* status by chain smoking, especially when it gives him a chance to challenge someone inconvenienced by it, a very negro trait, as we will see. This history needs to be written, and I will, for a suitable fee.

[5] I once attended a gathering of, I think, the Tradition, Family, Property groupuscle, where one of their elder statesmen held court—sort of an Allen Bloom crossed with Ernest Borgnine—surrounded by his acolytes, in a lawn chair, out on the lawn. "I smoke cigars to keep da fags away" he observed, to indulgent chuckles from the acolytes—certainly no fags, they—although neither seemed to notice it was the rest of the organization that was keeping them far away.

[6] Another example of America's absurd public Puritanism is the dearth of public lavatories or urinals, as Sigmund Freud observed when over here to accept an honorary degree, and finding himself and Jung dashing into a department store for a call of nature.

jumping a subway turnstile. Still, the reaction also seemed a bit over the top:

Misandrist bullshit.

These feminist idiots just need to be shot. Or less extreme punched square in the nose twice.

Yes, indeed, let us never be thought too extremist.

The question of dignified Aryan comportment in public called to mind the late series, *Mad Men*, which often addressed the issue, largely in the first seasons so as to set up the '60s atmos', which is the point here.

If, as the NRA likes to say, an armed society is a polite society, so is an Aryan society a polite society.[7] Conversely, if you want to create — or re-create — an Aryan society, you must first create a polite society.

Thus, in the epigraph above, taken from the pilot episode, Don Draper, '60s WASP Alpha Male, instructs privileged but clueless Alpha-wannabe Pete Campbell in the limits — admittedly, a bit subtle and not at all to subsequent feminist tastes — to how much you can paw and leer at your secretary (or, in this case, Don's secretary) and still be thought a nice — promotable — guy. Become a nuisance and you might "run" the place someday, but you'll never be "in charge," because you're . . . a jerk.[8]

---

[7] That an armed negro society is manifestly not polite, is another example of the ever present racial elephant in the room of conservative rhetoric. Speaking of "quality of life," few "mainstream" conservatives outside New York understand how Mayor Bloomberg's "liberal" anti-gun stance was compatible with his "conservative" stop and frisk policies, but some of us did.

[8] "She doesn't understand, I'm a jerk, sir." *MST3k*, Episode 406 — "Attack of the Giant Leeches."

In the very next episode, Don, after the usual drinking, whoring, and general Alpha Maleing,[9] gets in an elevator. Two men—jerks—get in later, and start telling a "blue" story, despite the presence of a lady. Don glares at them, and when he gets their attention, tells them to take their hats off, there are ladies present. At first, they shrug it off, but he keeps quietly looking down at them, and they sheepishly comply.[10]

Hypocrisy? Yes, but then hypocrisy is the compliment vice plays to virtue.

But can we imagine Don Draper, Roger Sterling, or indeed any manly White character of the pre-'80s manspreading? One might, though, imagine one of the younger, "hipper," more bumptiously Judiac characters, like the hapless Ginsberg, doing so, expressing the new, "let it all hang out" lifestyle promoted by the agents of the Frankfurt School.

More to the point, can one imagine Whittaker Chambers, William F. Buckley, Cardinal Spellman, or even Roy Cohn, manspreading? And yet it was these Evil Right-Wing White Men who ruled the supposed "golden age" today's lumpenright supposedly idealizes.

In fact, around that very time, as the '60s of *Mad Men* deflated into the "let it all hang out" *kulcha* of the '70s, Tom Wolfe had noticed the phenomenon, and gave it its classic—though unknown to these man-o-

---

[9] As John Slattery put it at the TCA Awards, "the show's message [is] drinking and smoking and whoring."

[10] Season 1, Episode 2, "Ladies Room." I can't recall any subway scenes, but has any show done more with elevators? Not likely. See "*Mad Men*'s Best Elevator Scenes," http://www.tv.com/news/mad-mens-best-elevator-scenes-28839/.

sphere types — analysis:[11]

> *That was the pimp look,* the look of hip and super-cool and so fine. The white bureaucrats, and the black ones,[12] too, walked in trying to look as earthy and rugged as they could, in order to be "with the people." They tried to walk in like football players, *like they had a keg of beer between their legs.* They rounded their shoulders over so it made their necks look bigger. They thickened up their voices and threw a few "mans" and "likes" and "digs" into their conversations. *When they sat down, they gave it that Honcho wide-open spread . . . as if the muscles in their thighs were so big and stud-like that they couldn't cross their legs all the way if they tried.*

As usual, the Real Men are fake men, trying to mock up a facsimile of manhood by imitating the negro. And as per usual, the negro is way ahead of them,

> But the pimp-style aristocrats had taken the manhood thing through so many numbers that it was beginning to come out through the other side. To them, by now, being hip was striking poses that were so cool, so languid, they were almost feminine. *It was like saying, "We've got masculinity to spare." We've been through so much shit, we're so confident of our manhood, we're so hip and so suave and wise in the ways of the street, that*

---

[11] Not that there's that much competition.

[12] Remember, 'tis is 1970. These guys are trying not to look like they're "acting white," or, as the saying then was, being "Uncle Toms." Today, government offices are filled with AA lottery winners who have no need to establish their 'cred.

we can afford to be refined and not sit around here trying to look like a bunch of stud brawlers. So they would not only cross their legs, they'd cross them further than a woman would. They would cross them so far, it looked like one leg was wrapped around the other one three or four times. One leg would seem to wrap around the other one and disappear in the back of the knee socket. . . . They would look like one of those supercool secretary birds that stand around on one long A-1 racer leg with everything else drawn up into a beautiful supercool little bunch of fluffy feathers at the top.[13]

Of course, few would want to follow Wolfe's analysis that far, and indeed, to do so would be to miss his larger point.[14] The White man never wins by imitating the negro, in pimp or gangsta mode, only by being himself; then the negro has a natural respect for the man of integrity, oneness, wholeness.

"They were so stiff, they swung," said techno legend [and suburban Detroit negro] Carl Craig, capturing the mysterious paradox of the German duo Kraftwerk. They made self-consciously

---

[13] "Mau-Mauing the Flak Catchers" in *Radical Chic & Mau-Mauing the Flak Catchers* (New York: Farrar, Straus & Giroux, 1970). "Both essays were later reprinted in Wolfe's collection *The Purple Decades*, indicating that he considered them among his best work" (Wikipedia).

[14] One notes in passing that the super-cool negro described here is also a thing of the past. Today's negro does not taunt by his elegance but by his revolting, sub-human appearance—"What you looking at?" The elegant appearance of the Fruit of Islam is a vestige of going the ofay one better, like Malcolm's earlier raspberry zoot suits.

"cold" songs about railways and autobahns and dressed like your stamp-collecting cousin, yet they're the founding fathers of all electronic dance music and a huge influence on hip-hop.[15]

Ultimately, it's not a gender issue, but also not just a racial one; it's a class issue. There has always been a segment of the White community that, consciously or not, emulated negro culture—they're called "White trash." Now, we may take their side on occasion, or support them to some extent, being as they are our fellow Whites, or our fellow men, but we help them best by leading and instructing them.

And speaking of instruction, if we want to revive, not just reminisce about, the good old days of White America, we need to start dressing the part.

As the man-o-sphere has forgotten, or never learned, but the actors on *Mad Men* knew, culture is, among other things, a matter of clothing and posture (the clothing often inducing the posture, such as the corsets originally devised for elderly generals sitting on horseback).

If you want to create an era, you must dress and take up the physical positions that arise within it, and that subsequently maintain it in being.

"Actors say that once you slip into your character's clothes, you become the character—and that couldn't be more true with *Mad Men*," Brie tells TVGuide.com. "You wear girdles and tight clothes you can't really breathe in that make you sit up straight. That alone is kind of oppressive

---

[15] "Most influential acts ever: 3. Kraftwerk," http://www.virginmedia.com/music/features/most-influential-acts.php?page=8.

and really makes you feel how these women were feeling at the time."[16]

So, you take a modern, "liberated" actress, put her in '50s-wear, and *voila*, no more Betty Friedan:

PC: I researched the time period, and both my parents grew up in the era, so I talk to them a lot about it. You also pick people brains on set because it's the little things.[17] *It's not so much the culture aspect, it's making sure to sit up straight, or if the line is, "I have to go to the bathroom," you don't say "I gotta go to the bathroom." You're very aware of how our language has changed 40 years later.*

EG: It was so proper compared to what it is today, so much more pronounced.

Q: *Does that carry over in your day-to-day life?*

PC: *I sit up straighter!*[18]

Mad Man creator Matthew Weiner, though raised in

---

[16] "*Mad Men* Star Reveals the Power of 'Oppressive' Wardrobe" by Gina DiNunno, August 7, 2009, online http://www.tvguide.com/news/mad-men-star-1008765/.

[17] As Vince Vega would say; like the chips with mayonnaise.

[18] "Interviews with *Mad Men*'s HBIC + those two beatniks idk" October 22nd, 2009, online http://ohnotheydidnt.livejournal.com/40351188.html#ixzz3b uflCGfk. Cf. my blogpost "Everyone on *Mad Men* is Polite, Not Just the Fags," http://jamesjomeara.blogspot.com/2009/11/everyone-on-mad-men-is-polite-not-just.html.

Beverly Hills,[19] brings a Coen Brothers Minnesota eye to it:

> And, you know, [Vincent Kartheiser, "Pete Campbell"] he's from Minnesota and as it turned out, *a lot of the cast was from the Midwest, and I think it was just a matter of manners. Just being raised with a certain kind of manners that fit the story.*

Really?

> Yeah, I think *it's something that hadn't been socialized out of them yet.* [Gee, Matt, I wonder who did that?] They weren't super casual. *They were polite, and it gave it a slightly period feeling.* But right away, he was up there to play Pete.[20]

Finally, one can't help but wonder if the guys alarmed by the demand to close their legs on their enormous packages[21] and batches[22] are, well, protest-

---

[19] Shown not manspreading at the Museum of Jewish Heritage, http://s.newsweek.com/sites/www.newsweek.com/files/styles/embedded_full/public/2015/04/04/4-4-15-matthew-weiner-mjh.jpg?itok=j1j-etXS.

[20] "*Mad Men's* Matthew Weiner Goes Deep on Vincent Kartheiser and Pete Campbell" by Jada Yuan, http://www.vulture.com/2014/04/mad-men-matthew-weiner-on-pete-campbell-vincent-kartheiser.html.

[21] "Weekend Discussion Thread: The Un-Sexiest Moment in a MSTed Movie": "Coleman Francis' enormous package all splayed in *Red Zone Cuba.*"

[22] "I have the MST3K version of *Boggy Creek II* and it's one of my favorites. It wasn't that bad except for the extremely tight jeans the main character wore (Crow's comment of his batch gets me every time)." Friday Video: *Boggy Creek II* MST3000 Style, http://www.ghosttheory.com/2011/06/03/

ing too much. Real men like Jon Hamm have no need of manspreading; the era's clothing and their natural endowment is sufficient for any territorial needs:

> Lately, the name Jon Hamm and the word "bulge" have become synonymous.
>
> A quick Google search for the *Mad Men* star will prove just that, and it seems the cast and crew of Hamm's hit AMC television series won't let him forget his past trouser offenses.
>
> According to the *New York Daily News'* Confidenti@l, an AMC insider said the "well-endowed" actor was instructed to wear underwear while filming certain scenes of the 1960s TV show, *due to the era's tight-fitting clothing.*
>
> *"This season takes place in the 1960s, where the pants are very tight and leave little to the imagination," said the source.*[23] *And it gets better: "Jon's impressive anatomy is so distracting that they politely insisted on underwear."*
>
> "When the promotional pictures came back the first few seasons, we had to work with them. Everyone was concerned about too much Christina Hendricks boob, but it's Jon that has the most to show. It's a good problem to have."

Counter-Currents/North American New Right,
June 3, 2015

---

friday-video-boggy-creek-ii-mst300-style.

[23] Perhaps, having adopted the homophobic negro's baggy pants, the Game Male now feels the need to spread out and reclaim his masculinity. Too bad. Now go home and get your fucking shinebox, and leave the rest of us alone.

MAD MEN JUMPS THE GEFILTE FISH, PART 1
MISSED CONGENIALITY

"Only act with Honourable Men: You can trust them and they you. Their honour is the best surety of their behaviour even in misunderstandings, for they always act having regard to what they are. Hence tis better to have a dispute with honourable people than to have a victory over dishonourable ones. You cannot treat with the ruined, for they have no hostages for rectitude. With them there is no true friendship, and their agreements are not binding, however stringent they may appear, because they have no feeling of honour. Never have to do with such men, for if honour does not restrain a man, virtue will not, since honour is the throne of rectitude"

— Baltasar Gracián's *The Art of Worldly Wisdom,* Aphorism #116

"When plunder becomes a way of life for a group of men in a society, over the course of time they create for themselves a legal system that authorizes it and a moral code that glorifies it."

— Frédéric Bastiat, 1850

While I was quite interested in *Mad Men* at the start, especially for its sense of fashion and décor — see my essay "Mad *Männerbund*?" above — I've been quite disappointed with the latest season, due to a perceptible ramping up of the "Judaics rule OK" factor; but the Memorial Day Weekend episode, involving a more than usually distasteful plot development—the partners of Sterling Cooper Draper Pryce agree to whore out fan-beloved office manager Joan to reel in a client—seems to have finally generated some general disgust and rebellion among the fans, to judge by the blogs etc., which articulate the more pertinent division between the True Believers, who acclaim the episode for "showing us just how awful and evil the times were" and Those Who See, who are "tired of plots about how totally evil [we] White folks are."

Coincidentally—if there are coincidences here in the Matrix—*The Occidental Observer* had an excellent review of a new movie that also reflects a new level of Judaic impudence—what we've called, using the Masonic terminology, The Revelation of the Method[1]—in the form of a new film called *Margin Call*.[2]

Short version: in 2008, a conspiracy of WASP bankers, led by Jeremy Irons (the blond East German terrorist in *Die Hard with a Vengeance*, more recently Pope

---

[1] See the work of Michael A. Hoffman II at his Revisionist History blog (http://www.revisionisthistory.org/) which also makes available his seminal book *Secret Societies and Psychological Warfare* (2001).

[2] http://www.theoccidentalobserver.net/2012/05/how-they-lie-to-us-the-film-margin-call. Even more recently, Kevin MacDonald discussed an article in the *Wall Street Journal* as evidence of a new level of "Jewish triumphalism regarding its domination of American culture" coupled with "strenuously resist[ing . . .] any mainstream public discussion of the fact that not only has their culture been taken away from White Americans, but the new culture of displacement-level immigration and multiculturalism inaugurated by the new Jewish elite is fundamentally opposed to their interests." http://www.theoccidentalobserver.net/2012/10/lee-siegel-exuding-jewish-triumphalism/.

Alexander in *The Borgias*), tried to take over the world, but were thwarted by a lone outsider, Jewish, natch. Yeah, that's what happened. Ah, I remember it well.

There's no conspiracy here—at least, not necessarily. It's the well-known Judaic ethnocentricity coupled with a double dose of ignorance: Judaic ignorance of White culture, and, thanks to previous anti-White culture-distortion, White ignorance of themselves.

"It's the little things" as Vince Vega would say. "They didn't know and wouldn't learn" as Charles Ryder's scout says.

For while The Revelation of the Method is a deliberate, albeit secret, strategy, what we have here, I suggest, is a different, and well-known, phenomenon: the Judaics have "jumped the shark."

In general, we can say that—just as TV critics have noted that popular shows will, *ipso facto*, be run year after year by greedy networks until, having run well past of original ideas, the writers will begin to "resort to stunts to retain viewer interest . . . such as 'it was all a dream' episodes, live episodes, lead actors playing guest characters, and putting [the] entire cast into a parody of some pop cultural event"[3]—we can also say

---

[3] Definition of "jumping the shark" at Urban Dictionary (http://www.urbandictionary.com/). The name stems from the episode of "Happy Days" where Fonzie jumped over a shark on water skis, which also illustrates our theme, since the "'50s nostalgia" show was gradually taken over by New York Jew Henry Winkler, originally a vaguely alien presence in the wholesome suburbs of Milwaukee ("For a show that in its early seasons depicted universally-relatable adolescent and family experiences against a backdrop of 1950s nostalgia, this incident marked an audacious, cartoonish turn towards attention-seeking gimmickry. Initially a supporting character, the faddish lionization of an increasingly superhuman Fonzie became the focus of *Happy Days*" says *Wikipedia,* http://en.wikipedia.org/wiki/Jump_ the_

that at some similar point, the mask will slip and the Judaic powers behind such shows will begin to reveal their agenda.

Once put forth by Jon Hein, the idea of jumping the shark spawned books and websites tracking such developments by fans of various shows, and "has subsequently broadened beyond television, indicating the moment in its evolution when a brand, design, or creative effort moves beyond the essential qualities that initially defined its success, beyond relevance or recovery."[4]

What causes this episode to "jump the shark" is the blatant inability to understand the collegiality, derived from the primitive Aryan *Männerbund*, that underlies, and makes possible, the great institutions of White civilization. Whereas for the Judaic, and the increasingly Judaicized TV audience, the only tie is what Marx called the "cash nexus."

Coincidentally, a real-life international firm, legal this time, blew up over the weekend, and the *New York Times'* post-mortem had this to say:

> "Because the partnership *lacks any shared cultural values* or history, *money becomes the core value holding the firm together*," said William Henderson, a law professor at Indiana University who studies law firms. "Money is weak glue."[5]

---

shark), and was created by Gary Marshall, a non-Judaic often mistaken, along with his sister Penny, for a Judaic since, as he boasts, "I grew up in the Bronx, and we had a lot of them." See "An Interview with the Cast of *Keeping Up With The Steins*," http://www.movieweb.com/news/an-interview-with-the-cast-of-keeping-up-with-the-steins.

[4] *Wikipedia*, ibid.

[5] http://dealbook.nytimes.com/2012/05/28/dewey-leboeuf-files-for-bankruptcy/?hp.

A bit later, a guest on *ZeroHedge* had this to say about the economy in general:

> In a society and culture that has lost its moral compass, [and thus] a culture of greed, self-serving lies, and corrupt vested interests, the word "evil" has lost its power. It has been reduced to a cartoonish label, a cynic's smarmy joke.

Like *Happy Days* post-shark?

> The Soviet Empire was evil, and President Reagan was mocked by "sophisticates" for labeling our global competitor evil. In the relativist terms of propaganda, the only difference between the U.S. and the U.S.S.R. were two letters; this is the mindset created by a reliance on propaganda. *There is no good or evil, there is only the paycheck* "earned" by serving one master or another. . . .
>
> Should we be surprised that the parasites in the media, academia, politics, and finance . . .

Hmm, I wonder who They might be?

> . . . support the evil that enables their own predation and exploitation? Of course not, for *self-service and self-justification are the ultimate American gods.*[6]

---

[6] "Guest Post: The Rot Runs Deep 1: The Federal Reserve Is A Parasitic Wealth Transfer Machine" by Charles Hugh Smith, August 26, 2012. Smith has an excellent blog, Of Two Minds, http://www.oftwominds.com/blog.html, that often runs such pieces, as we will soon see, where the parasites are triangulated

This is the general problem behind our current financial crisis, the so-called "fiscal cliff." The author went on to add at his own site:

Lobbyists aren't hired to understand the big picture, they're hired to secure a swollen river of *free money* for their vested-interest clients. Public unions, banks, Big Pharma, for-profit hospital chains, insurance companies, defense contractors, etc. don't care where the swag comes from or how it's skimmed, *they only care about getting their share of it.*

This describes not just the political battle between the 0.5% and the 99.5%, but the diverging interests of the various vested interests and Elites. It would be tidy if all the Elites were united, but as pressures build and systems are pushed to extremes, the interests of Elites diverge to the point that the system is pulled apart. *None of the Elites are willing to act in the best interests of the nation, and so their self-absorbed greed becomes a destructive force that cannot be controlled.*

The decline of the Roman Empire had this subtext. In Victorian England, the landed Elites who skimmed rents fought a political war with the Imperial "free trade" manufacturers who profited from the expansion of the Empire and the industrial workforce. The manufacturers won and the landed Nobility, though still immensely wealthy, took a back seat.[7]

Self-service may be designated our "ultimate god"

---

but never quite named.

[7] http://www.oftwominds.com/blogsept12/easy-stuff-gone8-12.html.

I suppose both prospectively and retrospectively; that is to say, ultimate as our final goal, but also, if you think about it, as something that only very recently became such. Were self-service, self-justification, and self-absorbed greed always our gods? And, as the Firesign Theatre famously asked, "who am us, anyway?"[8]

I'm calling "bullshit" or "shenanigans" on the whole idea. No, Mr. Weiner, I don't believe for a second that the senior partners of major Mad Ave. firms would tolerate for an instant the idea of whoring out a well-respected, long-serving employee to get an account.

Pete, sure, he's the designated sleazeball; precisely for his WASP background. In the very first episode, his treatment of female employees caused Don, the Alpha Male, to tell him he may get a corner office, but "everyone will hate you." As an outsider, he's allowed the Judaic role of "correcting" the errant WASP.

As for crazy, cranky Bert Cooper, we recall an early episode ("Nixon vs. Kennedy" Episode 1.12) where Pete, again, was the villain, trying out of pure spite to expose Don as an imposter (and, apparently, a battlefield deserter who could get the death penalty), leading to Bert's surprising, anticlimactic response: "Mr. Campbell, who cares?"

Who indeed? Not Bert, a WASP old-timer with a

---

[8] *How Can You Be in Two Places At Once When You're Not Anywhere At All*, Columbia Records, 1969, in answer to a patriotic chorus of "What Makes America Great": "Its spics and wops and niggers and kikes with noses as long as your arm! Its micks and chinks and gooks and geeks and honkies (Honk! Honk!) who never left the farm!" On the flip side, a disgruntled actor on the radio detective show "Nick Danger, Third Eye" dreams aloud of taking over and, among other things, having "no Jewish writers."

Samurai obsession—both cultures of honor, not money—but, apparently, more recently a devotee of crypto-Judaic Ayn Rand. Indeed, on Randian grounds, who cares, indeed, if Don is an imposter and a deserter, as long as he makes money for the firm?

But is this then a fair portrait of WASP values, or are they those of a Russian fanatic whose real life disciple wasn't Bert Cooper but Alan Greenspan, author of America's economic collapse?

> ALAN GREENSPAN: Well, remember that what an ideology is, is a conceptual framework with the way people deal with reality. Everyone has one. You have to—to exist, you need an ideology. The question is whether it is accurate or not. And what I'm saying to you is, yes, I found a flaw. I don't know how significant or permanent it is, but I've been very distressed by that fact.

> REP. HENRY WAXMAN: You found a flaw in the reality . . .

> ALAN GREENSPAN: Flaw in the model that I perceived is the critical functioning structure that defines how the world works, so to speak.

> REP. HENRY WAXMAN: In other words, you found that your view of the world, your ideology, was not right, it was not working?

> ALAN GREENSPAN: That is—precisely. No, that's precisely the reason I was shocked, because I had been going for 40 years or more with very considerable evidence that it was work-

ing exceptionally well.[9]

Did you catch that "everyone has one" bit? Straight out of Ayn Rand's "Philosophy: Who Needs It."[10] No, Mr. Greenspan, not everyone has an ideology, a crazy made up "rational" structure into which they spend 40 years trying to shoe-horn reality until finally giving up. Only, the Judaic. *Tikkun olam!*

The whole "idea" that "everyone is corrupt," "everyone is for sale," etc. is pure Frankfurt School drivel—authentic Judaic gibberish, to adapt Mel Brook's Judaic sneer at the wisdom of our pioneer forefathers[11]—in which the Judaic impudently imputes his own failing and obsessions onto the goy, and then contemns him for them.

The sexually obsessed Freud screams, "It's all about sex," the money obsessed Marx counters, "It's

---

[9] "Greenspan Admits 'Flaw' to Congress, Predicts More Economic Problems" from the PBS Newshour originally aired October 23, 2008, http://www.pbs.org/newshour/bb /business/july-dec08/crisishearing_10-23.html.

[10] "Philosophy: Who Needs It" by Ayn Rand. Address to the Graduating Class of the United States Military Academy at West Point, New York, March 6, 1974.

[11] A sample: http://youtu.be/ke5Mr5eCF2U. Of course, Mel would say it's "all a joke" if any White person objected, or to description of "the people of the land . . . you know, morons" (*am ha'aretz* or 'the people of the Land' is an old Talmudic insult). But like all Judaic "jokes," it's slow-acting cultural poison, rattling around in the heads of "these lovely children here today." According to the oh-so-unbiased Urban Dictionary, frontier gibberish is "currently used by members of the Tea Party in decrying the state of affairs in our nation. Characterized by longing for a return to the gold standard, Anglo-Saxon cultural supremacy, and the return of Johnny Carson to late-night television," while a commenter at YouTube adds "Sarah Palin's main stream media fantastic rant."

all about money," and the Frankfurters had the genius of combining both, through the efforts of the "dean" of the '60s — and well-paid CIA asset — Herbert Marcuse.[12]

Thus, confronted with the "ordeal of civility,"[13] the dirty little *Ostjude* turns the tables. Sure, he may pick his nose at the dinner table, but you, you stuffy WASP, secretly want to as well, and your fancy "culture" is just your dishonest "sublimation" of that desire.

Listen to how the well-indoctrinated Midwestern White boys of *Mystery Science Theater 3000* mock the very idea of dinner table civility; you may think it's "polite" or "civilized" but they know it's really a

---

[12] To paraphrase an Italian Rightist, he's the Left's Evola — only an idiot.

[13] See the invaluable *The Ordeal of Civility: Freud, Marx, Levi-Strauss, and the Jewish Struggle with Modernity* by John Murray Cuddihy (New York: Basic Books, 1974). Reviewed by a White Nationalist (http://library.flawlesslogic.com/yid.htm) under the wonderful title "Our Apoplectic Invaders Considered": "Freud described as 'sick' Gentile behavior that was, to us, healthy and necessary. But it was not out of mere misunderstanding that Freud came to his conclusions. Animosity toward Gentiles played no small part. . . . When Jews sneer that Gentiles are embarrassed by sex and need to be 'unmasked,' Cuddihy points out that what they're trying to do is strip all humanity to base commonalities in an effort to make their crude, uncivilized selves feel more acceptable, all the while rudely ignoring the evolved and genuine social need for Gentile conventions. The Gentile is left shamed and confused, convinced that he must "let it all hang out" if he is to achieve mental health. Freud is revealed as a clever Jew pleased with himself for having pulled the Gentile's pants down to point out to the assembled crowd that, like other mammals, this one's got genitalia. Cuddihy coolly returns the favor."

"seething caldron of angst."[14]

What I am suggesting here, as in my earlier piece on "The Fraud of Miss Jean Brodie"[15] — where we have the related phenomenon of a Leftist imagining a "fascist" sympathizer — is that the Jew, when "exposing" the WASP is really exposing himself (and keep your smutty Judaic giggling to yourself!). He has nothing to build his indictment on but himself, his own twisted view of the world and human nature, which he first impudently imputes to the WASP, then turns the tables by using the WASP's idea of fairness to convict the WASP, himself, of incivility!

We've see this, for example, in the Hollywood Nazi, believing himself to belong to a Master Race destined to "rule the world" and frothing with irrational genocidal hatred of all other races which must be exterminated; this caricature clearly corresponds to no known National Socialist of any significance, but is clearly the projection of the Hollywood Judaic, based on his delusional and genocidal ethnocentricity. To find the Frothing Nazi one must look at any random comment on foreign affairs by any "mainstream" Israeli or Christian Zionist politician; who, of course, are constantly warning us of the latest "New Hitler" *over there.*

---

[14] Parody of the short film *A Date with Your Family*, in which this '50s attempt to teach manners to the rising generation of juvies and immigrants like Da Fonze is now ridiculed by the MST3K with all the tropes of the Frankfurt School: Mother wants a career, Father's moving to Fire Island, brother is toking pot, sister is both pregnant and "dating a Negro." A similar "ordeal of civility" dynamic simmered beneath the *Seinfeld* scenes where George — supposedly Italian but for our purposes a Marrano — dined with fiancée Susan's parents (including a father who had a secret affair with John Cheever).

[15] http://www.counter-currents.com/2011/04/the-fraud-of-miss-jean-brodie/

Here too, the Judaics have jumped the shark; with *Inglourious Basterds*, audiences were sickened by the display of gleeful Jewish sadism, while responding to the "evil" Nazis as quite decent chaps.[16]

"You want the scent? Smell yourself."
                    —Hannibal Lechter, *Manhunter*

And to explain "how could the Germans do this" we have the too-famous "Milgram Experiment" which everyone "knows" proves we (viz., White folks) are all just itching to bow down to authority figures and start torturing innocent prisoners. As one critic writes of this absurd imposture:

> As if ordinary people were going to kill other people for 50 bucks. It's pure nonsense.
> They explain this behavior by saying people obey the authority. This is why they would obey the scientist of the experiment. Complete bullshit. Those people were not in the twilight zone. *They were in the USA in the '60s....*
> Those people would have immediately thought that they were committing a very grave crime and that it would not have been the authority of the scientist which would have protected them from being put in jail for murder. Which can lead you to the death penalty or, at best, being put in jail for the rest of your life. So, they would have very quickly ended this experiment. . . . And trying to make us believe that

---

[16] Trevor Lynch calls it "probably the most anti-Semitic movie ever released by Hollywood" in his *Trevor Lynch's White Nationalist Guide to the Movies*, ed. Greg Johnson (San Francisco: Counter-Currents, 2012).

someone would think "ok, you are a scientist. I respect your authority. Let's kill this guy" is ridiculous.

Needless to point out, Milgram was a Judaic, and explicitly conducted his "experiment" to "prove" the equally outlandish idea that the most educated, most civilized White people in the world would turn themselves over to demonic madmen and carry out "the worst crime in history."™ As the critic concludes:

> In fact, the real subject of this experiment is the *goy* who believe[s] this canard. By believing this ridiculous story because people with pompous titles at the television tells it's true he is the one who obey[s] blindly the authority as the experiment concludes.[17]

As for "it was the '60s," well, that's the whole point. The evil days before Judaics took things in hand. Once more, the same trope: a false story of the evil repressive White past is used to screw down the real, present (and future) Judaic domination. Freedom is indeed slavery.

And speaking of slavery, consider one final example, not a big movie about WWII but a half-assed TV movie about the Civil War: *CSA: The Confederate States of America* (produced by Spike Lee, but with the usual Judaic financing and producing "talent"). This shark-jumping farrago of nonsense is of course supposed to an "alternative" history anyway — what if the South won Gettysburg and then the war itself? — but the events dreamed up — the South takes over the North,

---

[17] See others by one "voerioc" at biglies.org.

and not just reinstates slavery there but *requires* slave ownership (how's that supposed to be financed? Sounds kind of like Obamacare), then heads off to conquer Central America, etc.—presupposes a level of ignorance about the motives of the South and, indeed, the mental state of the whole country, that is truly breath-taking, leaving one with the same question one had after one of George W. Bush's speeches: is he stupid, or does he think I am?

But then what is one to expect from a people who, as Norman Podhoretz famously stated, regard the Civil War as an event as "remote and as irrelevant as the War of the Roses?"[18]

Once again, Judaics draw on their own psyches (for indeed, was it not the North that was the expansionist,

------

[18] Philip Weiss, "Vidal stuck by dual loyalty charge against Podhoretzes to the end," http://mondoweiss.net/2012/10/vidal-stuck-by-dual-loyalty-charge-against-podhoretzes-to-the-end. Weiss adds this interesting observation about another culture-distorter: "I had this out with my old friend Norman Lear, who said 'you can't say "assimilated."' I said, 'Come on, *you started People for the American Way. Well, which are you? If you're not going to be an 'assimilated' American, then what are you?* Are you an Israeli who happens to be living here?'" Lear of course perpetrated the Archie Bunker caricature of White, working class Americans, despite an ignorance that led him to suggest, in the show's opening song, that they thought "we need a man like Herbert Hoover again"; White Americans then rewarded him with a ratings blockbuster that's still eulogized 50 years later; see Kevin MacDonald's "Norman Lear's 'All in the Family' Resurfaces," http://www.theoccidentalobserver.net/2012/11/norman-lears-all-in-the-family-resurfaces/, which also notes (without using the term) how the show eventually "jumped the shark" as Archie was relently and implausibly "Judaized," from adopting a Jewish girl to attending Seders to organizing a neighborhood group to protect synagogues!

totalitarian power, both internally and, once that was sewed up, going abroad to Latin America) to produce a distorted history, and Whites are ignorant enough to lap it up.[19]

As Francis Parker Yockey said about an earlier Judaic type, the Beatnik: "He believes in nothing and respects nothing because there is nothing within his range of vision worthy of respect or inspiring belief." Or as Schopenhauer said, "No man can see over his own head."[20]

And thus is our "modern world" produced: in which the past is denigrated and demonized as a cauldron of racism, sexism, slavery, oppression, mind control, etc.[21] while the supposedly "enlightened" present "presents" exactly those characteristics, and the public, continually "taught" how unhappy people must have been "back then," is increasingly unhappy and puzzled as to how that can be, and what can be done about it, since "going back" isn't an option.

A world in which hipsters watch movies like *CSA* on iPhones built by Chinese slaves.

The model, and goal, is the Israelization of the world, in which a land of state religion, heavily armed citizens, constant warfare, vast open air concentration camps, and women forced off sidewalks and spat on, is presented on billboards in New York subways as a

---

[19] You can enjoy some of the push-back from historically-informed and racially-conscious White Americans here: http://www.chimpout.com/forum/showthread.php?28634-nominate-the-most-anti-white-films-of-all-time-here/page2 and http://www.stormfront.org/forum/t509258-2/.

[20] Francis Parker Yockey, "The World in Flames," 1961.

[21] See, for example, Alex Kurtagic's discussion of the movie *Pleasantville* in "Those Awful 1950s," http://www.theoccidentalobserver.net/2012/09/those-awful-1950s/.

"civilization" to be protected against "the barbarians."[22]

Where is the true home of "racism, sexism, militarism and homophobia," America in the '50s or Israel today?[23]

A false image of the WASP past, constructed from scraps and rags provided by the Judaic spirit itself, has been set up as a Gorgon to bar the way back, while in the present the true Judaic spirit disports itself unchallenged; the only thing worse than being called a "conservative" or "reactionary" is being called an "anti-Semite."

This is the world constructed in *Mad Man*, where WASPS are conniving evildoers slowly being overcome by the forces of Good, in the form of Bob Dylan and a slow influx of Jewish copywriters.

---

[22] "A pro-Israeli poster comparing Muslims to barbarians will soon be displayed in New York City's subway stations following a US court order allowing such hate ads to be posted in public. The inflammatory billboard advertisement, which reads, 'In any war between the civilized man and the savage, support the civilized man. Support Israel, defeat Jihad,' has presumably been financed by radical conservative blog writer Pamela Geller and is to be installed at 10 different metro stops." "Anti-Islam posters to appear in NY subway stations," http://www.liveleak.com/view?i=f25_1348316039.

[23] In Chapter Two of *The Homo and the Negro*, "Homosexuality, 'Traditionalism,' & Really-Existing Tradition," I've discussed how homophobia in the Arab world is itself a creation of Western "modernity" which in turn is offered as the false "solution"; here again a fake past is constructed and then a fake solution offered. More generally, we see an even closer analogue in the cynically named "Arab Spring" in which peaceful, albeit authoritarian Arab states are designated as "failed states that support terrorism" in order to be torn apart by the USA and Israel and replaced by "free and democratic" states of unparalleled barbarism and violence.

To see what real WASP collegiality was, even when filmed through a Judeo-Marxist lens, no better specimen could be found than Otto Preminger's 1962 film, *Advise and Consent,* from Allen Drury's 1959 bestseller and, according to Peter Bogdanovich, "by far the best political movie ever made in this country."

AandC (not AMC) is essentially *Mad Men: The Movie,* with politics for advertising and gorgeous B&W photography for *Mad Men: TV's* '60s Cinerama color, plus the all the advantages of actually being filmed in Mad Men Time, such as a real Saul Bass title sequence rather than *MM: TV's* knockoff.

> "I thought they did a pretty good job portraying 1962."
> "Yeah, considering they made it in 1965."
> — *Mystery Science Theater 3000,* on *Red Zone Cuba*

Here's what IMDB has for a plot synopsis:

> A look behind the scenes at the wheeling and dealing that goes on in Washington to get things done. The dying President (Franchot Tone) nominates a controversial candidate (Henry Fonda as Robert A. Leffingwell) for Secretary of State. The film, based on real events, follows the public and private dealings as the Senate holds confirmation hearings on the nomination. Blackmail, smear tactics, political trade-offs and more highlight this movie. Senate majority leader Robert Munson of Michigan (Walter Pidgeon) tries to steer Leffingwell toward confirmation, with his initial roadblock being . . . Seabright "Seab" Cooley-SC (Charles Laughton). . . . . But Munson bypasses overly-ambitious Wyoming senator Fred Van Ackerman (George Grizzard)

to put Utah's Brigham "Brig" Anderson (Don Murray) in charge of the committee vetting of Leffingwell. . . . Van Ackermann sics a team of blackmailers on the bisexual Anderson in an attempt to ensure the nomination, even though Anderson, Munson, and the president know Leffingwell has provided perjured testimony about his past. Anderson travels to New York and assaults his old army lover outside a gay bar, returning to the Capitol to slit his own throat in his Senate office. Chastened by Anderson's suicide, Munson and Cooley agree to disagree in a "nice" way, and the full Senate vote on Leffingwell's nomination ends on a 47–47 tie since Munson has shamed Van Ackerman into walking out of the chamber before his name is called. Just as the voting ends, the Vicepresident Harley Hudson (Lew Ayres) is informed [of] the President's death. Knowing that Leffingwell has given false testimony under oath, Hudson refuses to honor his mentor's dying wish, stating that as president-apparent, he'll nominate his own choice for Secretary of State.

Wow, not much congeniality there! What a field day for one of our modern, Judaic or Judaic-inspired directors. Imagine what the Coen Brothers, or even Tim Robbins would do with this stuff.

But, and this is a large part of my point, those were different times. While we'll see that Preminger has some "socially conscious" cards to play, he is very careful—some critics at the time even finding him too careful—to present the Senate as, on balance, a bunch of flawed but honest individuals—all White men, of

course[24] — within a grand old institution — separation
of powers, "advise and consent," etc., based on a Con-
stitution which Preminger called "the finest machine
for governing yet invented," but which today the
"Right" mocks as a "piece of paper" (George W.) and
the "Left" denigrates as a charter of slavery.[25]

---

[24] There is one woman, Betty WHITE, and it's a real hoot to
see her in the role; sort of like the way her later co-star Ted
Knight shows up around the same time as a sheriff in *Psycho*. As
befitting the minor role of women here, she only appears once,
but it's a doozie, besting Van Ackerman in debate, thus demon-
strating his low status and qualifications for the *Männerbund* of
the Senate. Also befitting the times, she's a Republican from
Kansas, unlike today's coastal liberal harridans. She may be a
beard, lest the Senate seem too "Socratic"? It's interesting to note
that in various transcriptions on the internet, Munson's dress-
ing-down of Van Ackerman, which we'll soon quote, mentions
not "fanaticism" but to "Atticism." Truly, this Senate is a *Männerbund*. Other social outliers are Kennedy in-law Peter Lawford
as a JFK-like womanizer, thus presumably Catholic, and of
course the Mormon Brig Anderson. Gosh, it's almost like things
were "diverse" back then, isn't it?

[25] For perhaps more detail then you may wish on this fictional body politic, see the admittedly "long and self-indulgent"
analysis at "The Fictional Senate of Allen Drury's *Advise and
Consent*" by David Bratman (http://home.earthlink.net/
~dbratman/drury.html). Bratman also notes that "Pretty much
all of the dramatic events of the climax of *Advise and Consent* —
the suicide of a senator, the resignation and re-election of the
Majority leader, the censure of a senator, the death of a president
shortly before a major peace conference, the rejection by the Senate of an important nominee . . . — have thus actually happened.
Where Drury departs from reality is by having them all occur at
once, by speeding up the process many-fold, and in the political
spin he puts on his story." As we said about the equally true but
implausible events of *The Untouchables* (see Chapter 9 of *The Homo and the Negro*), both movies abide by Aristotle's dictum that
poetry is more true than history, since it narrates what ought to
have happened, unlike, we would add, Judaic inspired "fact

This was not yet "the" '60s, and why antagonize an establishment that's more or less going your way — desegregation, civil rights, etc.? Not until Vietnam split the elites would Washington *as such* become the target of the Left.

You'll notice that the kernel of the narrative is secret lives, just like *Mad Men*. The motor of the plot is Leffingwell's Hiss-like secret life, but the real focus becomes Brig Anderson. Just as Don needs to keep anyone from finding out that before accidentally killing the real Don Draper during the Korean War, he was just a hick named Dick, so Brig, played by DON Murray, needs to conceal a homosexual encounter during WWII.

The phalanx of Secret Service men who bound up the stairs of the Capitol and fan out across the Senate chamber in the wake of the President's death, in their dark, tight suits and hats, resemble the cast of *Mad Men* or perhaps *How to Succeed In Business*, a contemporaneous musical hit starring Bobby Morse, who now plays Bert Cooper.[26]

Van Ackerman is clearly the Pete Campbell of the Senate. In an interesting move, indicative of an earlier generation's objectivity, he's a funhouse McCarthy, now a Democrat giving speeches about need for a speedy peace treaty with the Russians to his local "committees" and employing an army of "researchers" to smear and blackmail anti-communists — Roy Cohn ret-conned as a homophobe. Like Campbell, he's youthful, brash, up-and-coming, and employs "research" to promote his ideas. They are the sleazy fu-

---

grubbing."

[26] Again, from MST3K's version of *Red Zone Cuba*, as black-suited Federal agents arrive on the scene: "The cast of *How to Succeed in Business* swarms in."

ture of their respective professions.[27]

But how differently they are handled! Campbell's blackmail attempt is airily dismissed by the Rand-promoting Senior Partner Bert Cooper with "Who cares?" After all, it's all about money, right?

By contrast, although he is guilty of not just attempted blackmail but even hounding a fellow Senator to his death, this is not what Van Ackerman finally must answer for. Rather, as the Majority Leader—standing in here for Cooper—tells him, "We tolerate about anything here. Fanaticism, prejudice, demagoguery, anything. That's what the Senate is for, to tolerate freedom. But you've dishonored us."

By the way, could today's Senate possibly be any more different? "Tolerate freedom" indeed! Imagine trying to maintain a viable political career after acquiring a reputation for fanaticism, prejudice, demagoguery, to say nothing of that ominous . . . *anything*. Former Minority Leader Trent Lott, for example, was hounded from the Senate after daring to praise not just "the old days" but their living representative: Sen. Strom Thurmond, in the heated political context of *a birthday party*. Not only from North Carolina but even President Pro Tem of the Senate, Strom is the exact double of *A&C*'s Sen. Seabright Cooley.[28]

---

[27] In another ret-con, he's given Wyoming to represent, while Utah Senator Brig's suicide recalls "the actual suicide of Senator Lester Hunt of Wyoming in 1954, and its treatment perhaps conditioned by Drury's own rumored homosexuality." See "*Advise and Consent* at 50" by Thomas Mallon, *New York Times*, June 25, 2009.

[28] See *Strom Thurmond's America* by Joseph Crespino (http://online.wsj.com/article/SB10000872396390444508504577 595433195614946.html). In that review the author notes that "Sen. Ted Kennedy appreciated the 'new' Thurmond, describing him as 'fair to all sides. That's the ideal that 'Sea' Cooley be-

While the Senate allows a lot that today is forbidden, there's one thing they won't stand for, that today is treated like a joke: honor. When's the last time anyone resigned over anything in Washington? Nothing's worth giving up the best gig around. When Van Ackerman protests that he acted for the good of the country (thus doing his job, as he sees it, like making money is the *Mad Men*'s job), the senior Senator from Michigan easily waves aside that excuse:

> Fortunately, our country always manages to survive patriots like you. We could introduce a resolution to censure and expel you. But we don't want Brig Anderson's tired old sin made public. Whatever it was. So we let you stay . . . if you want to.

When thus confronted, and suddenly aware that all of the Senate knows he has committed the one unpardonable sin—non-collegiality—Van Ackerman, finally achieving self-knowledge, does the decent thing and exiles himself from the body he has offended.

By contrast, Bert Cooper waives away Don's "sin" for no higher reason than because he's the best moneymaker in the firm, and Campbell's dismissal for incivility was never on the table—and eventually, he becomes a junior partner in the new firm—because he's the up and coming moneymaker; neither he, Cooper or even Don would even imagine resigning

---

trayed, as he finally admits to the Senate that his pursuit of Leffingwell was motivated by revenge for a personal slight, not national security." Needless to say, "fairness to all sides" is a dead letter to today's self-righteous PC Left; those who dare to disagree are mad or bad, and must be hounded to their death—sounds sort of like the way proto-Leftist Van Ackerman handles Brig.

out of a sense of honor.[29]

What then of Don's "tired old sin"? Whatever "it" was? There have been endless internet debates on exactly what Don's crime or crimes are. Desertion, treason, manslaughter, bigamy, in some combination, but what? Don usually calls it "desertion," but that may be just his own shorthand, or a cover story for an even more terrible crime.

> "They don't have a name for what he is."
> — Clarice Starling on Hannibal Lecter

> "Check first the ones rejected for having lied about criminal records, look for severe childhood disturbances associated with violence. Our Billy wasn't born a killer, Clarice. Oh no, he was made one through years of systematic abuse . . . Our Billy hates his own identity you see, he always has, and he thinks that makes him a transsexual. But his pathology is a thousand times more savage and more terrifying. He wants to be reborn you see. Our Billy wants to be reborn, Clarice. And he will be reborn."
> — Dr. Lecter on Buffalo Bill

An absurd comparison? Remember, Don is the Aryan Alpha Male as re-imagined by jealous little Hollywood Judaics, so any crime is possible. To the Judaic, the imagined "crimes" of the White world both justify his own behavior ("Hey, that's the dirty way you guys got to the top") and at the same time de-

---

[29] Don doesn't even know what acting on principle is. A few seasons back, Don's anti-smoking ad was written only after they had already lost Lucky Strike, and this season he's stunned to learn that his own industry took him seriously as an anti-smoking activist—and even worse, so did potential clients!

legitimize White society in its own, hyper-moralistic eyes ("How can we ever make amends for our horrible historical crimes?").

This is also the function of the cult of the Holocaust, which, being "the greatest evil ever committed," serves to simultaneously absolve Israel of any crime ("Hey, it's not like it's a Holocaust already!") while permanently indebting and inguilting the White world.[30]

Unless, and until, the White world learns to take Jonathan Bowden's advice and "just step over it."[31]

Of course, everything from *The Iliad* to *Jersey Shore* requires some suspension of disbelief, but the amorphousness of Don's "tired old sin" (unlike Brig's sharply delineated lapse, with its witnesses, letters, confrontations, and a laughable visit to a "gay bar" in New York City, complete with Hollywood Liberal Frank Sinatra showing his solidarity by licensing one single verse of a song to play on the jukebox, like a charity donation, etc.) suggests that it stands in for the total depravity of the WASP, historically guilty of all crimes, and hence, literally, capable of Munson's shuddery "anything" going forward.

In fact, I think I can tell you what Don's crime is: he is White, successful, and unashamed.

Counter-Currents/*North American New Right*,
November 9, 2012

---

[30] My own coinage, inspired by Dan Greaney's contribution of "embiggen" to *The Simpsons*.

[31] See Greg Johnson's "New Right vs. Old Right," *New Right vs. Old Right* (San Francisco: Counter-Currents, 2014), pp. 11, 24, 136.

THE COUNTRY OF THE BLIND

"Here Punch does a mean trick, very unworthy of his Satanic character. He tells the hangman that he has never been hanged before; and though he would be only too glad to be hanged he does not know which way to put his head into the loop, and asks the hangman to show him, which he does. And Punch suddenly fools the rope, and the hangman, who is the sole representative of legal vindication, is himself hanged! Hangman hanged, all law and authority defied, and every restraint annulled, Punch bursts out into triumphant song."

—Count Eric Stenbock[1]

"American politics used to be fun. Powerful men making decisions. Now it's just who has the most money and avoiding decisions."

—Comment at Classic Film and TV Café, February 2, 2012

In Part One of this essay, we suggested that just as long-running pop culture items, especially television series, will eventually reach a point where originality and creativity are displaced by clichés and gimmicks in a desperate attempt to maintain a profitable popularity—known colloquially as "jumping the shark"—so there is a related phenomenon, more directly inter-

---

[1] Count Eric Stenbock, *The Myth of Punch*, edited by David Tibet (London: Durtro Press, 1999).

esting to our readers, in which the Judaic background and intentions of such programs (and note the interesting use of the word "program" for such works) gradually comes to the fore and is apparent for all to see, at least those Those Who Can See—not unlike the Masonic idea of The Revelation of the Method.

To illustrate this idea, we looked at the increasingly Judaic content of the TV show *Mad Men*; not merely the introduction of more and more Jewish characters and themes—positively portrayed, of course—but also an increasingly negative and even contemptuous handling of the main WASP characters in what is, after all, supposed to be a look at the early 1960s, when, for good or evil, America was still an overwhelmingly White country.

In particular, we looked at the antepenultimate episode, in which we were expected to accept the idea that the partners in a Madison Avenue company, even one involved in the suspect business of advertising, would offer a partnership to their office manager, Joan, in return for her prostituting herself to obtain a client. We identified this as a typical Judaic strategy of attacking the validity of WASP authority structures by "revealing" them to be "really" selfish and corrupt; and since selfishness and corruption are inherently Judaic characteristics, also removing any objection to their admission.

Since such Judaic "inversion" has become a part of our cultural fabric, a Judaic-created and sustained reflex of cynicism, a kind of "automatic gainsaying" as Monty Python might call it, we tried to find a point of reference by contrasting the way WASP collegiality is portrayed in a film made at the time portrayed in *Mad Men*: Otto Preminger's film of Allen Drury's *Advise and Consent*. We chose the film because, although it takes place in the US Senate rather than an ad agency, the plot, characters, and especially actors suggest a kind of "doubling" of the later TV show. This method of discovering hidden meaning resembles what Dalí called his paranoiac-critical method in which images are mapped onto each other to create, or discover, new levels of significance. [2]

Although cynicism is the default attitude today, fans, to judge from the Internet blogs and chat, where shocked and distressed by the treatment of the popular *Mad Men* character Joan. Perhaps the writers had gone a little too far, perhaps "jumped the shark" too soon? It was this reaction that suggested to us that what we had here was an opportunity to see The Revelation of the Method in real time.

And indeed, with typical impudence, the writers decided to double down and, in the penultimate episode, have a somewhat less-liked character meet an even more grisly, but, as we shall see, even more revealing, fate.

1. "HAVEN'T HAD SO MUCH FUN SINCE THE CAYENNE PEPPER HIT THE FAN!"

By using Dalí's method of mapping *Advise and Consent* over *Mad Men*, we've seen how the cultural picture has been changed; the Judaic falsifies and cuts down to size the world of WASP collegiality, reimagining it as being as mean, venal, and materialistic as his own kind.

---

[2] "You were kind of a double kid, I bet, right? Huh? One kid with your old man, one kid with your mother. You're upper-middle class during the weeks, then you're droppin' your 'R's and you're hangin' in the big, bad Southie projects with your daddy, the fuckin' donkey on the weekends. I got that right?" — Dignam, *The Departed.*

Now let's look at the micro picture, how the Judaic distorts the models that society provides for the individual's spiritual development.

In my second look at *The Untouchables* I added to the idea of doubling the motif of sacrificial death.[3] Both motifs appear again now. *Advise and Consent* and this season of *Mad Men* each end in suicide. *Advise and Consent*'s Vice President Harley Hudson of Rhode Island doubles *Mad Men*'s Lane Pryce; but while in the film he also doubles the doomed Senator Brigham ("Brig") Anderson of Utah, offering the viewer a superior *modus vivendi*. In the TV show Harley's double, Pryce, is simply identified with Brig and given Brig's shameful death — rather than rising to the top, he kills himself in his office.

In *Advise and Consent*, an ailing, unnamed President of the United States nominates Robert A. Leffingwell as Secretary of State. The nomination is controversial, sparking a great deal of public debate and behind the scenes maneuvering. In the end, the Senate vote is tied. Vice President Harley Hudson refuses to break the tie; so the nomination fails. Then he informs them that the President has died during the vote. Hudson then leaves the Senate chamber with the Secret Service to take over as President.

Harley Hudson is the wimpy guy that stands up to the demagogue Senator Fred Van Ackerman of Wyoming, just as *Mad Men*'s Lane Pryce punches out Ackerman's sneaky, blackmailing double Pete Campbell. Harley is the first major character we meet in the film, though at first he hardly seems like one: a little man in a big chair down on the Senate floor, gazed at

---

[3] See "Of Costner, Corpses, and Conception: Mother's Day Meditations on *The Untouchables* and *The Big Chill*" in *The Homo and the Negro*.

with mild curiosity by foreign tourists who are confused as to how he can be President—of the Senate—
but not President; he's almost the last one we see,
striding off the floor after becoming, in fact, the—
new—President, surrounded by Secret Service agents,
after using his last act as Vice President—or rather,
refusal to act—to casually sweep aside all the clever
and fatal political machinations of the "more powerful" Senators.

Harley got where he is presumably through some
kind of convention compromise, rather like Joe Biden
of Delaware, and oddly enough, he seems to be popular with the ladies, at least in a "dear sweet boy" kind
of way. But his contribution to his party, and to his
country, will be far more significant.

He is what Jack Donovan calls "the runt"[4]—"He's
from one of those little states" explains the wife of the
French ambassador—again, like Biden—and is sometimes called "little Harley"—who, like Wallace in *The
Untouchables*,[5] makes up for his size with moral courage and a keen mind, supplying the parliamentary
maneuvers that saves the day—or, in this case, sets up
the next round of the cosmic spiral.

In the film-world, both Harley and Brig are eager to
do the President's bidding. They are loyal and have
been rewarded—Harley with the Vice Presidency,

---

[4] See Chapter Two of his *The Way of Men* (Milwaukee, Or.:
Dissonant Hum, 2012).

[5] See "'God, I'm with a heathen': The Rebirth of the *Männerbund* in Brian De Palma's *The Untouchables*" in *The Homo and
the Negro*, especially pp. 115–16. While, as I point out there,
Wallace's courage is shown when he enters what I call "full
Berserker mode" and attacks Capone's men with a shotgun,
still swinging it when the bullets run out, the outwardly more
placid nature of the Senate is shown by Harley's equivalent
outburst: "Hey, what got into Harley?"

Brig with a coveted committee chairmanship. But loyalty has its price—or its "Pryce." Harley seems to increasingly chafe under the confines of his position, openly mocking Senate Majority Leader Bob Munson of Michigan by confessing to a murder—another secret!—knowing he's not being listened to. For Brig—or "brig," the closet where this ex-Navy man is confined—his brief elevation to committee chairman results in his death, to avoid public exposure, but it also results in the downfall of his tormentors Senator Seabright "Seeb" Cooley of South Carolina and Van Ackerman—the old and the new.

Seeb is forced to publicly admit his vendetta against the President's nominee was largely personal, not patriotic, and Van Ackerman, despite "his kind of patriotism" is defeated, privately rebuked, and forced to flee chamber, perhaps to resign or found a peace institute. As we have seen, in the antepenultimate episode Joan is forced to commit moral suicide, but the partners triumph by getting the client. We might say that Joan is reborn as a partner, but it seems a hollow achievement—which is the Judaic's point.

In the film, we see a different, more uplifting kind of re-birth when Harley, Brig's double, reveals a final, last inch of inner hardness that Brig lacks.[6]

---

[6] Bogart's doctor during his final illness said, "When a man is sick, you get to know him. You find out whether he's made of soft wood or hard wood. I began to get fonder of Bogie with each visit. He was made of very hard wood indeed." See my essay on Bogart in *The Homo and the Negro*. One also thinks of Bunny Roger, WWII hero and legendary window decorator, who according to Nicky Halson's memoirs, *Redeeming Features*, was "was made of burnished metal. Physically very fit—I saw him run up mountains in Scotland, at the summit adjusting his makeup from a compact kept in his sporran—he was also fearless. As a captain in the Italian campaign, even if his tent was

At first, the movie seems to be about the President,[7] and whether his nominee, Leffingwell, will be confirmed. About a third of the way in, this Hiss/Chambers mummery is completely forgotten, having merely served to set up the real drama, Brig's secret homosexual fling in the Navy.[8]

Then Brig kills himself, and we spend the rest of the film on the floor of the Senate, dealing with Seeb and Van Ackerman. It's only when Van Ackerman's shame-filled flight from the chamber results in a tie vote that we remember Harley has been presiding, thwarting Ackerman and aiding Munson, and suddenly we realize that the whole movie was about him. Or at least, contrasting his manhood, his spiritual vi-

---

lined in mauve with gilt chairs, and his army overcoats altered to look like Garbo's redingotes, he was revered by his men for the number of Germans he shot—'some right up the arse'— and after the war even refused ever to set foot in Germany." See Chapter Five of *The Homo and the Negro*.

[7] In *Gabriel Over the White House*, which Jef Costello calls "the feel-good fascist movie of 1933" (http://www.counter-currents.com/2012/02/gangway-for-a-fuhrer-proto-fascist-cinema-of-the-great-depression/), the President, modeled on Franklin Roosevelt, dies after achieving his greatest aim, world peace under American hegemony. In our film, the President is also modeled after Roosevelt, tries to achieve world peace by nominating an ex-Communist as Secretary of State—Henry Fonda as Alger Hiss—but dies before even knowing the outcome of the ultimately failed vote. That president is played by Franchot Tone, who played the president's secretary and romantic rival in the earlier film.

[8] Audiences no doubt expected the movie to feature the big star, Henry Fonda, as Leffingwell, to continue to hold the field, but he completely disappears; just as that same year Hitchcock definitely upset audience expectations by killing off "the star," Janet Leigh, after spending the first third of the movie *Psycho* focusing on her story.

rility as Evola would call it, to Brig's.

The night before, two scenes ago, Brig and Harley had met on a flight from New York. As in *The Untouchables*, air travel, still relatively primitive in the early '60s, is a dangerous, liminal situation calling for shamanic powers; on *Mad Men*, it's been the scene of shape-shifting experiences for Don in Los Angles and Rome, and the schlubby Judaic who handles the TV accounts cultivates his LA sunburn as a status symbol.

While in New York, Brig had been confronting his homosexual past and Harley speechifying to a women's garden club. Our attention, of course, is on Brig, not Harley. He starts to impart some words of advice to Brig—is Harley another closeted homosexual, older and wiser, who recognizes Brig's problem?—but they are interrupted, and the moment passes. Instead, the next development we expected is Brig returning to his office and killing himself.

Back to the climax of the vote, and the movie. Here, things play out differently than they did in Brig's office. Van Ackerman is driven out, and when the vote draws to a close, Harley is privately informed that the President has died, making him, presumptively, the new chief executive. Like the shape-shifting corpses and sacrificial doubles we saw in *The Untouchables*, Harley, unlike Brig, has succeeded in escaping death by handing it to another—he does not die for the President, the President dies for him.[9]

The vote ties, and Harley refuses to cast a vote; un-

---

[9] In Derek Marlowe's *A Dandy in Aspic* the death of the titular *double* agent is referenced in code as "the passing of the buck" which suggests President Truman's slogan, "the buck stops here." The sequence here echoes the inaugural speech of President Kennedy—another FDR double—and eerily foreshadows his own, possibly sacrificial death.

aware of the President's death, the Senators assume he has been defeated, stabbed in the back by his Vice President. As in *The Untouchables,* in the climactic scene when the juries are switched at the last minute and Capone's lawyer changes his plea, chaos breaks out (although no one, like Robert de Niro's Capone, starts swinging punches).

Seeb, who loves drama and upsetting apple carts more than winning, sits back, hands on big belly, smiling like a Buddha: "Something's haaaaa-pened" he drawls to Munson.

Indeed, something has happened; the only thing that really happens, all else being illusion: the change of cosmic cycles, engineered by the Superior Man.

As René Guénon points out frequently, death is always and only simultaneous rebirth at another level, whether of the individual or of a whole cosmic cycle; a principle reflected in the saying "The King is dead, long live the King." The same, somewhat undemocratic principle underlies the idea of Presidential succession.[10]

The little man has revealed himself as having been, if not ostentatiously "in charge" all along, like the preening Munson and the uppity Van Ackerman, certainly as the one with the final say. He is the *chakravartin,* The King of the World who, motionless in the center (the Senate rotunda) causes all things to move.

---

[10] A year or so after the film, this would be impressed on the public mind by Lyndon Johnson's very publicly witnessed taking of the oath of office in mid-flight from Dallas, a photograph of which was speedily sent round the wire services. Throughout the Cold War there was some paranoia about being "leaderless" for even a moment, even if the President were under anesthesia during dental treatment, perhaps culminating in Alexander Haig's bizarre announcement that he was "in charge" after Reagan's shooting.

Seeb Cooley, looking on in pleased wonderment, drawls, "I haven't had so much fun since the cayenne pepper hit the fan"—an interesting, Southern-fried version of the traditional symbol of the fan, or swastika, whiling at the center of the universe, dispersing the various states of being.

Brig undertakes all sorts of actions—agreeing to head the Leffingwell committee, which upsets Ackerman and leads to the whole disaster, trying to confront his accusers in Washington and New York, ultimately failing and committing the last act, suicide.

But Harley, like the *chakravartin* or the Taoist Superior Man, acts effectively by taking no action at all—"The Vice President [like all realized men, he has no personality, and so refers to himself in the third person] will not exercise his Constitutional privilege to break this tie with an affirmative vote."

As he makes his stately exit from the chamber, he deigns to explain himself to Munson: "I'd prefer to name my own Secretary of State."

Like Bartleby, he prefers not to . . . accept the choice presented to him from the dead hand of the past. Unlike Brig, who allowed his past to control him, Harley will choose for himself. As Carl Schmitt would say, that one is the sovereign, who can choose during the State of Exception.

One might feel that what handicaps Brig, or simply manifests the same flaw in a different way, is his religious faith. As Nietzsche's favorite historian, and Basel colleague, Jacob Burckhardt wrote regarding the moral sense of the great figures of the Renaissance, who served as the models for the Nietzschean *Übermensch*:

[They] show, in respect to religion, a quality

which is common in youthful natures. Distinguishing keenly between good and evil, *they yet are conscious of no sin. Every disturbance of their inward harmony they feel themselves able to make good out of the plastic resources of their own nature, and therefore they feel no repentance.* The need of salvation thus becomes felt more and more dimly, while the ambitions and the intellectual activity of the present either shut out altogether every thought of a world to come, or else caused it to assume a poetic instead of a dogmatic form.[11]

Those who feel capable of making good any felt lack through "the plastic resources of their own nature" have no need of salvation from outside; those who do, are ripe for Christianity . . . and destruction.

Thus we see the meaning of the title: there are those who *Advise*—Harley to Brig, Harley to the Senate, ultimately, Harley to himself—and those who merely *Consent*—as Brig allows his enemies to control him through his past.[12]

---

[11] *The Civilization of the Renaissance in Italy*, Part Six: Morality and Religion, Chapter 5, "Religion and the Spirit of the Renaissance."

[12] Though not particularly Nietzschean, the actor, Lew Ayres, is an interesting choice, according to this blog:

A whole generation was haunted by Lew Ayres reaching out for that butterfly in the final scene of one of the worthier Best Picture Oscar winners (*All Quiet on the Western Front*), but Ayres himself suffered for taking the lesson of that anti-World War One movie to heart. At the onset of World War Two, Ayres declared himself a conscientious objector and suffered savage criticism from all sides. He served honorably in the war as a medic, but refused to put himself in any situation where he would have to kill another human being. After the war,

"YOU'LL HANG HIGHER THAN HAMAN!"

Today's *Mad Men*, though set in the same era as *Advise and Consent*, portrays a very different world — in fact, an inversion. *Mad Men's* sacrificial suicide victim, Lane Pryce, is a re-writing of Harley Hudson, giving him Brig's secret crime and failed resolution.

Pryce, who first appeared in Season Two as a financial overseer when Sterling Cooper was sold to a British conglomerate, comes to like living in New York rather than London, and especially rather than New Delhi, which is where he's to be transferred "as a reward" for a job well done. So, in the Season Three finale, he conspires with Bert, Roger, and Don to steal the firm and its clients out from under his old masters. He is rewarded with a name on the door, but this requires him to pay in equity to the firm. Now in Season Five we learn that he did so by selling his British stock

---

Ayres' film career petered out, and he made most of his living from television guest appearances. As an older man, he devoted himself to a labor of love, a documentary about Eastern religion called *Altars of the East* (1955), which eventually grew into *Altars of the World* (1976), an intelligent, judicious look at faith of all kinds. In that engrossing film, Ayres shows that all religions are based around the precept that we must love our neighbors as ourselves, do unto others as you would have done unto you, and so forth. He spends a lot of time weighing the pros and cons of each faith; by the end, Buddhism wins out as the best and most challenging of disciplines. . . . This was a man so touchingly sensitive that the infamously grudge-holding Joan Crawford ended a book of interviews with Roy Newquist on a pained *mea culpa* for yelling at Ayres when he was late to the set of a movie they were making.

http://www.slantmagazine.com/house/2008/06/5-for-the-day-lew-ayres/

portfolio; since the new firm hasn't prospered as he expected, he faces a ruinous tax assessment. Pryce forges Don's signature on a company check to give himself a "thirteen day loan" but is tripped up when the Christmas bonuses are delayed. Desperate for the money, he cashes the check anyway. Bert eventually finds the cancelled check while bumbling around the office and informs Don; confronted, Pryce asserts that the money is his anyway since he made the firm possible, for which he's never been rewarded, but Don demands that Pryce resign. Pryce sets his affairs in order and goes home to read up on suicide. He attempts to asphyxiate himself in the Jaguar his wife bought him in expectation of the bonus, but the notoriously unreliable British car fails to start. Pryce eventually hangs himself on his office door, leaving a *pro forma* suicide note that reveals his contempt for the partners.

This time, the sin is financial, and its discovery by Bert/Seeb leads not to his elevation to higher office but his hanging in his old office. Rather than triumphing, Pryce will be dragged down from his high position (unlike Harley who strides down in his new estate) and suicided (like Brig).

Such reversals are characteristically Judaic. The Old Testament is a sequence of stories where the "hero" is lauded for overcoming his superior through lying, cheating, and other trickery, from Jacob, whose very name means "supplanter," to the much lionized David, who comes to prominence by cheating on the field of honor.[13] The impudent, "you got a problem

---

[13] Sanctimonious Sunday school stories never inform the ignorant that David and Goliath are supposed to meet in single combat, but David "wins" by cheating—he knocks out Goliath from a distance with his slingshot, then runs up and cuts off

with that" style puts the lie to any notion that "sharp dealing" is an "irrational stereotype."[14]

What is perhaps uniquely Judaic is not merely the reversal, but also the subsequent gloating: overdone, vulgar, and never-ending. Here the *locus classicus* is the story of Esther, where Haman is not just thwarted, but hanged on the very gallows he had planned for Mordecai; moreover, the Hebrews then embark on another of their "justified" orgies of genocide, and have continued to "celebrate" their "victory" to this day in the carnivalesque feast of Purim.[15]

---

his head. A comparison of the scruples and conscience shown by Arjuna on the Field of Duty in the Bhagavad-Gita displays all we need to know about how different the moral atmosphere of each race is.

[14] Recent archeologists have been forced to conclude that the Judaic invasion of Canaan actually never happened, leading one to speculate about the nature of a people that would ascribe a fictitious genocide to themselves, and then boast about it.

[15] Even today, the Judaic Left, so quick to call for "civility" on the part of the Neo-Judaic Right, celebrates its election victory by demanding mass murder:

> The Blaze reported Tuesday. "These Tea Bag bas***ds who by the way, I just wish they would all just go away—or, like in Passover, I just wish there was an angel of the Lord that would pass over—instead of killing the first born in all the households of Egypt just wipe out all the Tea Baggers," he said. Malloy, perhaps securing his place as the most unhinged liberal hatemonger on radio, continued by suggesting the "angel" decapitate everyone in the Tea Party. "Just, you know, the terrible swift sword, just lop their heads off," he added, while making exaggerated "swishing" sounds.— "Libtalker Mike Malloy calls for beheading of conservatives" (http://www.examiner.com/video/libtalker-mike-malloy-calls-for-beheading-of-conservatives).

In fact, when I said dragged down then suicided, I might better have said dragged down and then hung up, or hanged, as Pryce's means of suicide is Haman's mode of execution.

Which is an interesting change: while Brig's suicide is relatively discreet, in the style of the times—a gun shot heard from his office washroom, oddly resembling the suicide of General Jack Ripper in the next year's *Dr. Strangelove*—Lane's end is given the whole Judaic "c'mon, don't be hypocritically squeamish" treatment, his body taken down by the three partners and laid out on a sofa in some crass version of Christ's deposition from the cross, his face ashen, in a sequence that shocked viewers almost as much as the treatment of Joan (though excellently performed by Jared Harris).

I think the change of method is significant. The writers are not just reversing Harley's character, leaving the WASP with no honorable fate, but even going further: reversing no less than the ur-archetype of the Aryan, Wotan himself.

You may recall that I noted a moment in *The Untouchables* when Malone frightens a crook into cooperation by holding another crook against the wall—only Malone and Ness know he's already dead, a corpse—and shooting his head off. I connected this to the shamanic motif, in particular the mythological trope of Wotan and the Runes. Wotan hangs himself for three days to learn the meaning of the Runes; Malone hangs up the corpse to learn the meaning of the code in Capone's logbooks.

But what is the threat Malone delivers to the corpse?

"You'll hang higher than Haman!"

I would suggest, then, that Haman and Wotan are symbolic opposites, that rather than Wotan, who acquires knowledge through self-hanging, Haman is the clever plotter, foiled and then "hoist by his own petard" by the trickier Hebrew. And in this episode of *Mad Men*, not only is Harley's character reconfigured into a failure and suicide, his attributes of Superior Man or *chakravartin* are reconfigured as a failed Wotan.

I've already identified Harley and Wallace as what Jack Donovan would call "runts" who make up for their size with knowledge — Wallace of the tax code, Harley of parliamentary procedure. Both can thus be further identified specifically with Wotan as well.

Wallace is hanged in the elevator by Frank Nitti, while I would characterized the rostrum of the Senate, from which Harley presides, then steps down from when exiting to take the oath of office, as being similar to the World Tree that Wotan hangs from — like the World Tree, it is the World Center to which all attention is directed, like radii — from the floor, to the visitors' gallery, to the public, including the Oval Office, listening intently to the vote on radio — though perhaps not literally located in the middle of the chamber; it is probably made of wood, and like both the Tree and Wallace's elevator, it is a liminal location where one can move up and down.[16]

---

[16] Just as we first meet Harley through the conversation of the ambassadors' wives, commenting on his apparent irrelevance, now near the end another background conversation gives us a clue about him. As the Secret Service men climb the stairs there's an odd little bit of business in the background; a tour guide explaining a painting to some tourists notes that when the British surrendered Washington refused to accept Cornwallis's sword, because it was proffered by an officer below him in rank. One thinks perhaps this is to prepare us for

As we might expect, Pryce's Wotan-attributes are largely negative. His rune-lore, in the form of ad agency accounting, is just a bunch of contemptible tricks and schemes, unworthy of a noble, first annoying the American partners when he acts as auditor for the new British owners, then proving his runt-worth by devising a plan for them to steal the firm out from under the limeys.[17]

His confrontation with Pete over the latter's bungling of a potential client—which we now know Pryce desperately needed to make the firm profitable to hide his embezzlement—unlike Harley's with Ackerman, involves no intellectual cleverness at all but just fisticuffs—admittedly, seeing Pete "get plastered," as William F. Buckley threatened to do to Gore Vidal, was rather cathartic for the audience, but still beneath the dignity of a supposed Wotan. And his attempt to cover his mounting debts—caused by his vanity-driven partnership buy-in, as well as his inability to discipline his wife's spending—by forging a payout from the company becomes, like Brig's secret, his ruination.

Finally, Pryce's attempt to read up on suicide methods—acquire knowledge of the runes—becomes a macabre joke. Deciding to asphyxiate himself in the Jaguar whose purchase by his wife was the last straw, the lousy car fails to start. Here, in his apartment building's garage—another liminal setting, this time

---

the presidential succession, or to strike the right note of aristocratic politics and rank. But did the British military band not play, on that occasion, a tune called—"The World Turn'd Upside Down"? His stately descent and exit from the Senate, presumably to take up residence in the White House, also suggests Wotan's "Entrance into Valhalla" from *Das Rheingold*.

[17] We know this is a mean trick, because the British company is headed by the guy who was so nice to *über*-Judaic Fran Drescher as *The Nanny*: "Oh, Mr. Sheffieeeeeeeeeeld!"

underground—the Wotan motifs are become more obvious, preparing us for the most obvious one of all, the hanging.

Pryce settles in the car and then *snaps his spectacles in half*. Now, as someone who wears glasses himself, I found this odd; is this a common thing for myopic suicides I asked myself? Online discussions of the scene, which others found odd as well, suggested this was to demonstrate "no turning back." We, on the other hand, might connect it with the breaking of Wotan's staff, here a self-inflicted wound, rather than, as in the opera *Siegfried*, reflecting the triumph of Siegfried over the dead hand of fate (and itself a reversal of Wotan's action in *Die Walküre*).

But more importantly, the failure of the car to start forces Pryce to try to decipher the manual—more rune-reading—and to do so fashions a crude monocle. I think it is pretty clear that we are to see him, if only subliminally, or collective-unconsciously, as the one-eyed Wotan.[18]

Since everything is reversing, Pryce moves *from* his one-eyed state *to* his hanged state. His corpse's face, grey, ashen, suggests the World Tree, which is an ash—as the Norns sing, Wotan's rash act of tearing off a branch to fashion his spear has killed the Tree:

The wound, as time grew old,
wasted the life of the wood;
sere, leafless and stricken, fast faded the tree . . .

In fact, a few seasons back, Pryce confronted, or rather, was confronted by, his own father, a bearded gi-

---

[18] Not to be confused with the Illuminati's Eye of Horus. For an exhaustive look at the one-eyed motif thrust at us continuously in pop culture, see the website vigilantcitizen.com.

ant of a man who struck him down with . . . his stick. We see that not only is the age of Wotan in the past, but it is a past that Pryce, like Brig, will never be able to overcome, and which will eventually lead to his death.

The final Judaic touch: when Bert reads Pryce's suicide note, he exclaims in amazement:

"It's just boilerplate!"

Oy, the WASP with his fancy-schmancy woids and cultcha, he's ultimately just another Hollow Man. Rather than acquiring knowledge of the runes and gifting it to others, Pryce communicates nothing.

So we see that for our age, *Mad Men* has fashioned for us a Purim Masquerade, featuring Wotan/Harley, an empty suit stuffed like a Guy Fawkes dummy who, rather than provide an inspiring contrast to Brig, will wind up as not merely as a failure, but a pathetic one. The 1960s world of Aryan men of honor, presented without question even by a Liberal progressive like Otto Preminger, has in *Mad Men* been replaced, or "unmasked" as the producers would say—though that's typical Judaic double-talk since it's really, like Purim, more a deceptive masking than an revelatory unmasking—as a world of money-grubbing chiselers and failures, soon to be replaced by another race that's better at, and more honest about, the grubbing.[19]

They have, we might say, "revoked the Ninth."[20]

---

[19] In his essay on "The Myth of Punch," Count Stenbock notes (p. 11) that in *Tom Jones* Fielding—a Brit, like Pryce— refers to "Punch and his merry wife Joan." Is this ultimate source for the symbolic linking of Pryce/Punch and the married but decidedly un-merry Joan?

[20] In Mann's *Doctor Faustus: The Life of the German Composer*

TWILIGHT OF THE *MAD MEN*

Finally, let's round up some stray doubles to illustrate the many levels of synchronicity found between the movie and the later TV show, and the kinds of significance that may emerge as we contemplate them.

Adrian Leverkühn, Told by a Friend (1947) the titular composer, aware that his brain is rotting from syphilis, decides to avenge himself on German, that is, Western Culture by using his twelve-tone musical system to "revoke the Ninth Symphony." We could say that it is atonalism, a Judaic invention if ever they were one, and their own unique "contribution" to Western music, is indeed musical syphilis.

Arnold Schoenberg was so incensed at Leverkühn's appropriation of "his" methods that he forced Mann to include a note in subsequent additions, admitting the Schoenberg's "ownership" of the method. Of course, as Coomaraswamy often pointed out, no Aryan would ever claim "ownership" of an idea; truth is the property of all, while it is precisely error that is individual and "original."

Mann's relation to the Jews is typically hard to pin down; *Faustus* contains some excoriating portraits of Judaics, from crooked musical promoters to the "polyhistor" Dr. Chaim Breisacher, who delights in confounding his Prussian hosts with a version of true "conservatism" more barbaric than any Soviet (and based, some speculate, on the equally confounding Julius Evola; the Left's Evola, Herbert Marcuse, quotes Leverkühn's revocation in his "Essay on Liberation" —with approval, of course. He also explicitly ties it to the music of "sensuous" and "frightening immediacy" born in "the dark continent" and "deep South," in that once-fashionable, now cringe-inducing way of the Peter Paul and Mary Liberal).

On the other hand, Mann makes sure, right at the start, to have his narrator apologize for having to mention such distasteful characters, to point out that, literally, some of his best friends are Jews, and to explicitly point out "that I was never able to agree fully with our Führer and his paladins." His narrator, who loses his job but nevertheless stays in Germany, unlike Mann, is no doubt an attempt to atone for his having spent the war in sunny LA.

As Evola says, although principles are principles, context matters, and the same principle in a different setting will yield different results. In their climactic confrontation in *Advise and Consent*, where Munson rejects Ackerman's blackmailing methods and forces him to flee the chamber, we see that Munson/Ackerman/Brig (though already dead) doubles in *Mad Men* Bert's rejection of Campbell's attempt to blackmail Don (who "really" died in Korea), but elsewhere things are otherwise. When the dynamic is Munson versus Cooley, it's Robert Morse's Bert that doubles Charles Laughton's Sen. Seeb Cooley, with his eccentric, old fashioned ways, stout figure and goatee suggesting Cooley's cornpone Senator.

And Walter Pidgeon's Majority Leader Munson, slick old silver fox and ladies' man, will then be Bert's "junior" partner, Roger Sterling. *Sterling* represents the *Silver Age* of the WASP, still on top thanks to Daddy's clients (the firm was Sterling Cooper because of his father, Bert's partner) but sinking fast and not knowing just why. His WASP rule is as phony as Don's identity, both the targets of a pushy, knowing new generation of Judaics.

That sinking away is seen in the opening animation. From day one, fans have speculated that it's Don, finally jumping out the window; this enabled the producers to distract attention from Pryce turning out to be the suicide in the penultimate episode. Don won't kill himself, at least not until the very last scene; as the embodiment of Aryan evil, he must be shown to destroy all who come in contact with him—the "real" Don Draper as well as his "real" brother, and Pryce's wife, we'll see, will blame Don for his death—thus providing the narrative motor. Like that real life embodiment of Aryan Evil, Hitler, he can't die until his usefulness is over; hence the "Hitler is alive" rumors and "New Hitler" enemies.

Like Majority Leader Munson, or John McCain, Sterling "represents the majority," but since *Mad Men* is a later, Judaic version, Sterling's character fades into the background rather than taking the lead like Munson, played as a man behind the times with his drinking, smoking, and adultery — even saddled with a Jewish ex-wife, a typical method of Judaic infiltration — despite all of which he is probably the fans' favorite.

But who is *Advise and Consent*'s equivalent of Don Draper? Although the Homosexual Secret plot was given to Sal, who was exposed and tossed aside, not only by the firm but by the show's Judaic producers,[21] here it serves as the main plot line, or McGuffin, and that makes handsome Sen. Anderson the designated Don Draper character. Remember, Don has become a Family Man as well this season, like Sen. Anderson.

Just as the partners seem OK with Draper's "secret" as long as he makes money for them, so the Senators in the supposedly "homophobic" 1950s are OK with Brig — remember, "We don't want Brig Anderson's tired old sin made public, whatever it was" — since he is an honorable man. His private life is just that, private. Even the "swinging" is subtle, almost courtly, even with the Kennedy-esque "ladies man" played by Peter Lawford. Aryan Man keeps all things in propor-

---

[21] Sal is the only original Sterling Cooper employee who has never shown up again; I guess he was useful to show up the era's supposed homophobia — don't get me started on the absurd idea that no one knew art departments were *the* place for homos, just ask Andy Warhol — but ugh, who wants to bring up the *faygelehs* again, right Matt? Come to think of it, that fey chap Don hired from Season Two seems to have disappeared after outing himself, too; talk about exploitation!

tion and proper bounds; they almost resemble the chicks described in *American Psycho*:

> DAVID VAN PATTEN: A good personality consists of a chick with a little hard body, who will satisfy all sexual demands *without being too slutty about it.*

Ironically, in the days before the Senate became a Millionaire's Club, a forced life away from home and family means everyone has what Pete Campbell can only dream of: a hotel suite in the City, away from the wife.[22] And further irony: it's the closeted Brig that, like big phony Don, lives the "ideal" family life with wife and kids (albeit with one divorce and one fake marriage).

Just to tidy things up, Joan on *Mad Men* is also a double for Brig in *Advise and Consent*; he's bisexual, remember? As a woman, she is as much an outsider as Brig Anderson, the homosexual and presumptive Mormon (he's from Utah and named "Brigham"). She has her secrets as well, including an affair with Roger, which flared up once after her marriage and produced her child, while her husband was in the Army in Viet Nam, just as Brig's secret was a single homosexual encounter while serving at Pearl Harbor.

But while the Senators stand against Van Ackerman and behind Brig and his sexual secret, though perhaps too late, the name partners at SCDP them-

---

[22] Alain Daniélou made the controversial statement (a Traditionalist "gaffe" like talking about the truth of the caste system) that the British Raj collapsed because Victorian morality required wives to come out to live with their husbands in the Civil Service, thus destroying the sexually free-wheeling *Männerbund.*

selves conspire with Peter/Van Ackerman against Joan/Brig and force her to become a prostitute, just as Brig's long lost partner is now a blackmailing escort in, of course, Sal's New York homosexual underworld.[23] I wonder if he ever meets up with Sal?

ENVOI

But let us leave this sad state of affairs and ask ourselves, finally, Bert Cooper's earlier question: "Who cares?" So what, if an Aryan culture of honor has been replaced by a swarming mob of hucksters?[24]

---

[23] Another of Preminger's cinematic firsts is the first portrayal of a "gay bar" in an American movie. The opening credits indicate a song is to appear, and it turns out to be one verse of a song specially composed to appear on the jukebox during this scene, in a performance grudgingly contributed by Frank Sinatra — remember when he was a "Hollywood Liberal"? The scene itself is so filled with stereotypes of pudgy old losers and young Four Freshmen types in J. Crew pullovers that it makes the gay preppy spy gang in *Agent for H.A.R.M.* or the "gay high school Secret Service" in *Red Zone Cuba* look like a grisly killing machine. Preminger, Progressive Film Maker or Pseudo-Highbrow Exploitation Hack? It's always so hard to tell with the Left.

[24] In *Why America Failed: The Roots of Imperial Decline* (New York: Wiley, 2012), Morris Berman insists that America has always been a "nation of hustlers" on the make. From this perhaps deeper perspective, the New England WASP, with his Puritan moralism that never really seemed to conflict with making a buck — one thinks of the Quaker owners of the Pequod in *Moby Dick* — was always just a crypto-Judaic at heart. Interestingly for an academic Leftist, he has kind words for the cavalier culture of the South. He now lives in Mexico. See the interview on Alternet (http://www.alternet.org/story/154453/why_the_american_empire_was_destined_to_collapse), and especially the review at Second Vermont Republic (http://vermontrepublic.org/why-america-failed). This would be in accord with the general European Right view of America

For an answer, let us turn again to Burckhardt, who describes what the men of the Renaissance found to be "the strongest bulwark against evil":

> The highly gifted man of that day thought to find it in the sentiment of honor. This is that enigmatic *mixture of conscience and egotism* which often survives in the modern man after he has lost, whether by his own fault or not, faith, love, and hope.

The "mixture" is what the Judaic attacks, impudently claiming that conscience is just a cover for, or really is, egotism. By the time of these Mad Men, only egotism is left.

> This sense of honor is compatible with much selfishness and great vices, and may be the victim of astonishing illusions;

As in Munson's speech, quoted in Part One, about all the vices the Senate tolerates in the name of free speech.

> yet, nevertheless, *all the noble elements that are left in the wreck of a character may gather around it, and from this fountain may draw new strength.*

This is where Brig failed the test. But in the real '60s of the film, we still had the likes of Harley as a model, or even Seeb Cooley, who confesses his guilt and ascends to take Harley's place as the Senate's presiding officer.

---

as essentially a Judaic creation in the New World, destined to destroy white homelands.

It has become, in a far wider sense than is commonly believed, a decisive test of conduct in the minds of the cultivated Europeans of our own day, and many of those who yet hold faithfully by religion and morality are unconsciously guided by this feeling in the gravest decisions of their lives. . . . It is certainly not always easy, in treating of the Italian of this period, to distinguish this sense of honor from the passion for fame, into which, indeed, it easily passes. Yet the two sentiments are essentially different.[25]

Discussing this passage in the context of "a history of the United States in the twentieth century," John Lukacs adds that in our time:

[T]he difference—indeed, the discrepancy—between fame and honor has become so great that in the character of presidents, and in those of public figures in all kinds of endeavor, the passion for fame has well-nigh obliterated the now remote and ancient sense of honor.[26]

Counter-Currents/*North American New Right*,
December 19 & 20, 2012

---

[25] Part Six: Morality and Religion, Chapter 2, "Morality and Immorality."

[26] John Lukacs, *Outgrowing Democracy: A History of the United States in the Twentieth Century* (Garden City, N.Y.: Doubleday, 1984), p. 288.

"THIS IS A SHIRTSLEEVE OPERATION":
JUDAIC CRYPSIS IN THE
FINAL SEASON OF *MAD MEN*

CADDY DANNY NOONAN (working-class Irish American): "I planned to go to law school after I graduated, but it looks like my folks won't have enough money to put me through college."

JUDGE SMAILS (rich WASP): "Well, the world needs ditch diggers, too."

— *Caddyshack* (Harold Ramis, 1980)

If Steve Sailer can leverage his high school days to psychoanalyze Matt Weiner's *Mad Men*,[1] then I can ransack my own past for inside dope!

A lot of people don't believe me about how much of what you see on TV today is driven by great-grandpa not getting into Los Angeles Country Club and therefore having to found Hillcrest Country Club, but listen to the creator of *Mad Men* instead, and he'll say the same thing.

. . . Here's Matthew Weiner, son of a leading neurologist and a lawyer who stopped practic-

---

[1] "Matthew Weiner on How *Mad Men* Is Driven by His Resentment of WASP Country Clubs" by Steve Sailer, April 6, 2015, http://www.unz.com/isteve/matthew-weiner-on-how-mad-men-is-driven-by-his-resentment-of-wasp-country-clubs/.

ing to keep house, yet it still drives him nuts that Jews were a minority at Harvard School for Boys. He gets up in the morning and goes to work to get revenge for that.

I had thought—and surely some others did too—that *Mad Men* was gearing up to tell us the typical triumphalist story of how advertising, like everything else, got so much better after the Jews overcame, through sheer talent, those mean, artificial, upward mobility and free market distorting WASP barricades and took over.[2] From the very first episode:

ROGER STERLING: "Have we ever hired a Jew?"

DON DRAPER: "Not on my watch."[3]

The chosen vehicle seemed to be one Ginsberg, a pushy, loud, sarcastic, badly dressed, and hairy chap, but he was too bumptious, too explicitly Jewish ("born in Auschwitz" no less!) to really be suitable.[4] Exit Ginsberg, in a straitjacket.

As a sort-of fan, I've never been interested in Don Draper, neither his family life (such as it is) and romances, nor his absurd backstory,[5] nor the travails of

---

[2] Surely you've noticed how much better books, movies, and education have gotten, right?

[3] "Smoke Gets In Your Eyes."

[4] See the classic study of Jewish bumptiousness, John Murray Cuddihy, *The Ordeal of Civility: Freud, Marx, Levi-Strauss, and the Jewish Struggle With Modernity* (New York: Basic Books, 1975).

[5] How many people know by now that Don Draper is really Dick Whitman (= dick + white man), guilty of desertion and manslaughter, both capital crimes? After all, we all know every successful WASP is a big old phony, right? Does everyone

the plucky ladies striving to survive in a "man's world," but rather in the constant, almost comical shifting of partners and organizational alignments, almost as if Sterling Cooper were less a WASP ad agency and more a Temporary Autonomous Zone or even a pack of Wild Boys.

As Season 7 progressed, first founder Bert Cooper died, and then the loveable firm known under various forms of Sterling Cooper[6] itself died, or rather, "died and went to advertising heaven," as Jim Hobart, the head of their new owners, McCann Erikson, smugly — and falsely — tells them. (He is in advertising, after all).[7]

Now, from the start, McCann has been the Eye of Mordor for everyone, the monolithic bureaucratic nightmare (that somehow manages, after all, to be the leading creative force in advertising — go figure!). But there's something a little off about how McCann is presented to us.

It started a few episodes back, when we learned why former SCP-er Ken Cosgrove was "shot out of there like a cannon."

---

agree with Bert: "Mr. Campbell, who cares?"

[6] To paraphrase Murray Kempton on Nixon's law firm, Mudge Rose, one always thought of it as something like Sterling, Cooper, Nasty, Brutish and Short. This HuffPost article on "Ken Cosgrove" gives and unintentionally funny account of the convoluted family tree of SCP (http://www.huffingtonpost.com/darryl-woodard/mad-men-that-wily-kenny-c_b_7035980.html).

[7] Bloggers have noted that Don's doomed last ditch pitch to McCann, to set up SCP as a rump LA outfit called SC West, shows that he agrees with me: he has the most fun not drinking, whoring, or even pitching slogans, but shuffling organizational charts.

"I'm not Irish. I'm not Catholic. I read books."

Where did that come from? Were illiterate Irish Catholics running Madison Ave. all these years?[8] It can't come from Weiner's high school angst; Sailer again:

> As a Catholic from the flatlands of the Valley, I was always kind of baffled by the dominant ethnic animus of the region, *which was hostility toward WASPs, because we Catholics didn't count* because we weren't very competitive or interesting. If you are a white Catholic in Boston, say, that's potentially pretty interesting, but being a white Catholic in Los Angeles is just kind of random. If you are in Southie you can blame it on the Potato Famine, but if you are growing up in Sherman Oaks, it probably suggests that some of your ancestors had some good sense and spare change.

What suddenly made everything fall into place was this ominous line:

"This is a shirtsleeve operation."

It's a motif that has been popping up throughout the season, as bloggers have noted:

Ferg mentions that McCann "is a shirtsleeve op-

---

[8] "Really, Ken Cosgrove? You didn't fit in at McCann because 'I'm not Irish. I'm not Catholic. And I can read'? Don't be showing your face in Boston with an attitude like that!" Robin Abrahams, "*Mad Men* Analyzed: Looking the Part," *Boston Globe*, April 6, 2015.

eration—we want you to relax." While that might be the stated purpose of the agency's dress code, the more obvious upshot *is to make everyone look the same, like drones in a hive. Don is taken aback by the worker-bee effect when he steps into a conference room packed with white-shirted men buzzing about before the Miller meeting.* "Is this every creative director in the agency?" Don asks Ted Chaough. No, it's only half of them, explains Ted, who's wearing shirtsleeves.[9]

Elsewhere, such as the season premiere:

> Don seems trapped. *He's in his shirtsleeves, gripping a cup of lunch-cart coffee. This is work.*[10]

And in a later episode:

> Indeed, the opening shots of this scene feel like they depict an alternate universe, one in which Don and Betty somehow found enough contentment to raise their kids together. *He works the blender in his shirtsleeves.*[11]

Shirtsleeves = work, yeah, I get it. But it brings something else to mind, at least for me. Years ago, I worked at a "top ten" law firm in New York. Now, one of the "top three" firms would be a classic "white

---

[9] *Onion AV Club*, http://www.avclub.com/tvclub/mad-men-lost-horizon-218897.

[10] *Rolling Stone*, http://www.rollingstone.com/tv/recaps/mad-men-season-premiere-recap-is-that-all-there-is-20150405#ixzz3ZGnA3cYf.

[11] *Onion AV Club*, http://www.avclub.com/tvclub/mad-men-new-business-217919.

shoe" Wall Street outfit; this one, always just making
the Top Ten list, had been founded to service a unique
niche: lawyers and clients who would otherwise quali-
fy for one of those Top Three firms, but for one thing:
they were Jews — or Irish.

This, in other words, was the place for the smart
Jewish lawyers that the white shoe lawyers wouldn't
hire; but they still didn't get the white shoe clients;
they got the clients that, however rich, the white shoe
firms wouldn't touch — other Jews.

One such category was the big department stores;
lots of money, but not the sort of peddlers you wanted
hanging around in your offices.

Indeed, the aforementioned bit of "anti-Semitic"
dialogue from Roger and Don starts off an episode
where Sterling Cooper considers the lucrative but
shady idea of taking on a Jewish department store as a
client. (Don, however, decides to take on the owner,
Rachel Menken, as his latest paramour.)

Anyway, it was made clear to me that this was "a
shirtsleeve firm" where associates were expected to
show up in suit and tie, and then dispense with the
jacket (perhaps even the tie) while getting down to
work. A complete suit and tie was seen only on such
rare occasions as a client conference or a court appearance.

Now, the Irish presence gradually become compar-
atively small (we'll get to that bit again), so this was
definitely a "Jewish firm" as Roger's worried comment shows he would understand the phrase: "Most
of the Jews work for Jewish firms."

So it seems clear to me that Weiner is using the
"Irish Catholic" McCann firm to pantomime the Jewish takeover of the ad world; the firm is, we might say,
"implicitly Jewish." And so the WASP firm of SCP is

reconfigured as plucky upstarts, and thus "implicitly" Jewish as well.

A veritable Purim festival of disguise and misdirection! The Jewish self-image, creative upstarts against monolithic conformity, is played out against McCann, while the later encrypts the real world takeover of WASP professions by upstart Jews. As always, there are two sides, both good for the Jews.

Encrypting SCP as Jewish takes various forms with each character. Ken Cosgrove, we've seen, describes himself, and thus his colleagues, as not Irish, not Catholic, but not as WASP either, since the WASP of course is a blonde dolt who eschews books in favor of athletics and gentlemanly C's.

Though from Vermont, he, like scion of Old New York Pete Campbell, performs as a Woody Allen-style "real New York Jew" when dealing with the Midwesterners of GM, unable to drive and injuring himself several times, including losing an eye while hunting.[12]

Joan, her role diminished at McCann and subject to sexual harassment, strikes back by threatening them with the ACLU and Betty Friedan, both Judaic weapons.

I've previously discussed Bert Cooper as a pseudo-WASP whose cult of Ayn Rand and blithe unconcern about Don's false identity (observing in passing, like a good neo-con, that America was built by men with worse backgrounds) type him as already Judaic, so it's no surprise when his ghost reappears in Don's car to

---

[12] Lane Pryce, though a Brit, is a runty little pencil-pusher who breaks his glasses and has to squint through one eye before hanging himself, as I discuss in "*Mad Men* Jumps the Gefilte Fish: The Country of the Blind," above; this is an inversion of the Wotan meme, like hanging of Haman during Purim, and continues here.

give him advice (more on Don's drive later).

More interestingly, the other name partner (actually, his father's name, because as we all know, WASP privilege is unearned, right?), Roger Sterling, though alive, is given a ghostly entrance—playing a creepy, Carnival of Souls type organ in the abandoned SCP offices—for a session of drunken advice giving of his own; to Peggy, as always Don's younger/female surrogate. We also recall his Jewish wife, making him an "OK goy."

But before dealing with Don and Peggy, I have to step back a bit and observe that we've seen this film before.[13]

Back in the late '70s, two Jewish directors (Harold Ramis and John Landis) inaugurated the "slobs vs. snobs" genre with *Animal House* and *Caddyshack*. In both, we see the same meme: stuffy but lame WASP institutions and authority figures (Faber College, Dean Wormer; Bushwood Country Club, Judge Smails) get their comeuppance from feisty, take no prisoners upstarts. In both cases, the upstarts, though white ethnics, are implicitly enacting the Jewish revolt against the WASP.[14]

---

[13] Mad Manhunter? Will Graham: [stunned realization] "You've seen these films! Haven't *you*, my man?" See my "Thanks for Watching: Awakening Through Repetition in *Groundhog Day, Point of Terror*, and *Manhunter*, Part 1," http://www.counter-currents.com/2013/10/thanks-for-watching-part-1/ and "Phil and Will: Awakening Through Repetition in *Groundhog Day, Point of Terror*, and *Manhunter*, Part 2," http://www.counter-currents.com/2013/12/awakening-through-repetition-part-2/

[14] *Caddyshack* sides with the Irish caddies and Carl the Groundskeeper (Bill Murray, presumably Irish). Al Cevic, played Rodney Dangerfield (Jacob Cohen), deflects attention as the obvious Hebraic invader; see his entry on Jew or Not Jew,

Back to SCP, whose abandoned and self-trashed offices recall both the slob hangout of Delta House, and the post-parade carnage of *Animal House*, as well as Carl the Groundskeeper's shack, and the presumed wreckage of the golf club after Carl sets off the dynamite.

Here, Peggy, still dressed up for work, is cajoled into joining Roger for drinks and boozy reminiscences, ultimately advising her to stop trying to make the men she works with comfortable, and shake things up instead. We next see Peggy arriving at McCann, carrying her office in a box, like the boys being evicted from Delta House: hungover, smoking, bloodshot eyes behind dark glasses, and carrying Bert Cooper's Japanese tentacle porn etching for her office: the smart-ass slob, ready to take on The Man.

So where's Don? Don was so terrified by that vision of men working in white shirts that he took off out west, like some buttoned-down Jack Kerouac, ultimately picking up a hippie with a guitar, taking him to St. Paul. A Bob Dylan (Zimmerman) in reverse, perhaps taking Don to meet the Coen Brothers?[15]

His escape makes his *Animal House doppelgänger*

---

http://www.jewornotjew.com/profile.jsp?ID=411. In *Animal House*, the boys are dolts and Delta House is explicitly not "the Jewish house" but as in all such films they are "street smart" enough to sabotage the Homecoming Parade, and the only other Jewish character mentioned, the late Fawn Leibowitz of Emily Dickinson College, is atypical as well, being from the Midwest. Chapter President Hoover rather resembles Ken Cosgrove.

[15] In the midseason premiere, Don was already trying to pass for Jewish (he's already changed his name, right?), claiming honorary Jewish cred at Rachel Menken's *shiva* by saying "I've lived in New York a long time." They don't buy it, and close the door in his face.

obvious: Don Draper is, of course, Daniel "D" Day, careening off in a stolen cop car, "whereabouts unknown."[16]

He's played by Bruce *McGill*, which reminds us of *Mad Men*'s AMC stablemate (donkey to *Mad Men*'s thoroughbred,[17] *Better Call Saul*. Here we see the final stage of the process: while the lowest tier and night law schools used to be full of scrappy working class Irish kids, their numbers have been diluted almost to nothing by Jews; now Jimmy McGill (graduate of the University of American Samoa Correspondence School of Law) has to change his name to Saul Goodman: "My real name's McGill. The Jew thing I just do for the homeboys. They all want a pipe-hitting member of the tribe, so to speak."[18]

What once was cryptic, now is mandatory.

Counter-Currents/*North American New Right*,
May 5, 2015

---

[16] Peggy has D-Day's dark glasses, and as for his motorcycle, when Roger convinces her to roller skate around the abandoned offices, we are reminded of her tricking a rival agency some time ago by riding a motorcycle around in circles in an abandoned warehouse.

[17] In the Season 4 episode of *AbFab* titled "Donkey," Patsy points out that you don't stable two thoroughbreds together, but with a donkey, otherwise they'd kick the shit out of each other.

[18] Wikipedia, http://en.wikipedia.org/wiki/Saul_Goodman

Don Draper's Last Diddle:
The Finale of *Mad Men*

Having followed *Mad Men* from the start, with initial enthusiasm gradually tempered by the increasingly exposed triumphalist agenda, I found the series finale, pumped (or pimped) by the network as "the end of an era," to be somewhat forced, mainly by the perceived need to top network stablemate *Breaking Bad*'s finale, as well as Weiner's earlier series, *The Sopranos*.[1]

Written and directed by creator (or "show runner" as the kids say) Matthew Weiner, we can assume the final result accurately reflects his intentions. Most of the cast get their conventional happy endings;[2] and then there's Don.

The idea of Don dropping out, heading circuitously to Esalen, and achieving some kind of enlightenment (or Satori, as Jack Kerouac would say) seemed unlike-

---

[1] By contrast, I found the *Breaking Bad* finale far more involving, despite having only caught up with the series in a post-finale marathon. See "Breaking Badge: *Touch of Evil* through the Lens of *Breaking Bad*," http://www.counter-currents.com/2015/01/breaking-badge/.

[2] As one blogger writes: "In fact, it was a happy ending for everyone. Everyone that is, except for poor Betty. Because Betty is dead" (http://uproxx.com/tv/2015/05/matthew-weiners-mad-men-ending-was-genius-or-terrible-or-both/2/). Betty, the Nordic Ice Princess, continues to be Weiner's punching bag to the end. At least she appeared; Sal Romano, the closeted homosexual who was fired for refusing to sleep with a client (for which Joan was rewarded with a partnership) disappeared entirely. Internet legend has it that the actor, Bryan Batt, angered Weiner by questioning his son's acting ability (i.e., ethnic networking).

ly, but the immediate cut to the iconic "I'd like to teach the world to sing . . ." Coke ad tells us that Don simply found a great idea, and headed back to New York to rejoin the rat race as the renewed Alpha Male. As one blogger writes:

> He broke all his vows. He scandalized his child. He took another man's name. He didn't want to end up like that guy [at the encounter group], and there's only one way he could redeem himself . . . by making something great, and by God, he did. He made the "I'd Like to Buy the World a Coke" ad. He *is* the ultimate con man!

Ultimate, because he finally fooled even us. What we thought was Don quitting his new but conformist job and taking a trek across America to finally "find himself" turned out to be just another attempt to find an angle for a new ad.[3]

And that, of course, has been the theme all along: the Aryan Man as a fake, a con, no better than, and rightly supplanted by, the Judaic Man.

To correctly understand the final sequence, we need to remind ourselves that Weiner seems to belong to an earlier, or perhaps just richer and more conservative, stratum of the Judaic Cultural Left;[4] he hates hippies.[5]

---

[3] As Roger says to Don's outraged boss, "He does this all the time." Coca-Cola was the account that boss dangled before Don to sweeten the idea of selling out SCP to McCann. There's an ironic call-back in this episode when Joan samples "coke" for the first time.

[4] See Steve Sailer's analysis of Weiner and his resentments quoted in my "'This is a shirtsleeve operation': Judaic Crypsis in the Final Season of *Mad Men*," above.

[5] See Betty's encounter with the East Village squatters, Rog-

But these aren't hippies, they are "human potential" pods, and that's an eminently approved Judaic
cultural weapon.

Thus, Esalen teaches Don the new cultural value of
the "real me." Weiner I suppose thinks Don doesn't
get it—Don still never reveals his "secret"; but perhaps he doesn't so much pervert the idea as recognize
its inherent phoniness.

In "There and Then: Personal and Memorial Reflections on Alan Watts (1915–1973)"[6] I wrote:

> More generally, Watts was certainly aware of,
> and opposed to, the way the need, as he per-
> ceived it, to "relax" was being perverted into
> "let it all hang out." As Columbus and Rice note,
> though he was one of the founders of Esalen and
> the "human potential movement" himself, he
> was by no means supporter of "Beat" culture. *In
> My Own Way* has a stunning rejoinder to all that
> hot tub chatter:
>
>> In such situations people will invariably say
>> to me, "Oh come on, Alan, we haven't yet
>> seen *the real you*." To which I can only reply,
>> "Well, look, I am right here, all of me, and if
>> you can't see you must question your own
>> sensitivity" (p. 209)

---

er's at the commune his daughter runs away to, and Weiner's
own creepy kid enlisting to go to 'Nam. The numerous hints
that led some viewers to speculate there would be a Manson
encounter got a call back when the Esalen receptionist tells him
no one will pick him up hitchhiking, and "you can thank Manson for that."

   [6] http://www.counter-currents.com/2015/01/there-
and-then/

He goes on to point out that the "metaphysical assumptions" of such hot-tub chatter, superficially "friendly" but really aimed to tear down and re-build, are "ill-digested Darwin and Freud, with a touch of Jesus" and are, moreover, "demonstrably false."

As the references to Freud and Jesus show, Watts was, like many if not most intellectuals of his era, somewhat "jew-wise." His opposition to the Businessman and Priest is implicitly Aryan and Traditionalist, and so is his opposition to their fake alternative, the Slob.[7]

Another layer is revealed, however, when we focus on how that last shot of Don moves from satori to a smug smirk. I could not but recall the enigmatic ending of Sergio Leone's *Once Upon a Time in America* (a fitting alternate title for *Mad Men*).

As we've noted before, Weiner uses *Mad Men* to reverse or parody various Aryan themes,[8] as the series

---

[7] In "'This is a shirtsleeve operation,'" above, I identify Peggy as a new convert to the future slob culture of the post-*Caddyshack* world where snobs like Don are uncool. As Cuddihy and MacDonald have documented, the Jew, when "emancipated" by Napoleon, was faced with a cruel fate: how to "make it" outside the self-imposed ghetto, when by common consent he was dirty, stinky, ugly, and uncouth. The answer, from Freud and others, such as the Frankfurt School, was to create a "counter-culture" in which such features as bathing, neatness, and politeness were denigrated as "un-natural," "repressive," etc., and their opposites lauded as "natural," "authentic," and "free." As a result, people fly from the up-tight to the un-couth, and the Jew wins every time.

[8] For example, the parody of Odin's hanging and one-eyedness in the fate of Lane Pryce in "The Country of the Blind," above.

dramatized the slow displacement of the Aryan Male; and we can see *Mad Men* as subverting Leone's film as well. De Niro's smile, as he dreams away in a 1932 New York opium den after his attempt to save his best friend's life ends in his death and his own flight into pseudonymous hiding, has been interpreted as hinting that all the events chronologically after that—but before it, in cinematic time—are a dream.[9]

Speaking of reversals, Leone supposedly made the film as a riposte to Hollywood's version of Italian gangsters, starring *Godfather II's* De Niro but creating a far more sophisticated merger of past and present than the rather simple back-and-forth of Coppola's film. Like the Judaic producers who recut the movie to make it easier for audiences to understand, Weiner has made *Mad Men* in strict chronological order.

The major reversal is that in Leone's film it is James Woods' Max who supposedly dies, burned beyond recognition, while in Weiner's series it is the original Don Draper that Our Don accidentally incinerates and takes the identity of. Typically, Weiner projects the Judaic crypsis onto the hapless Dick Whitman (dick + white man).

It is Max, the Jewish gangster from the Bronx, who engineered the hoax, reversing and exploiting De Niro's plan—never try to trick the Trickster!—and transforms himself into the echt-WASP Commerce Secretary Bailey, to whose Long Island mansion De Niro (I can't call him, as Leone does, "Noodles"; why do Italian directors give Americans such odd names?) is summoned to hear Bailey summarize the story arc of *Mad Men*:

---

[9] See my remarks in "Essential Films . . . and Others," http://www.counter-currents.com/2015/02/essential-films-and-others/.

I took away your whole life from you. I've been living in your place. I took everything. I took your money. I took your girl. All I left for you was years of grief over having killed me. Now, why don't you shoot?

And unlike De Niro, Don does shoot . . . a TV commercial.

The commercial pounds home the irony of "the real thing." One thinks, of course, of Henry James' tale, in which downscaled aristocrats discover they are unsuitable as artist models; they just don't look real when posing as aristos, unlike the lower class models. The Judaic theme can be played either way: the WASP aristos are just fake anyway, or, the Judaic can do a better job in the role.

Ultimately, the grin is as American as apple pie. Whether Leone or Weiner knows it, the *locus classicus* is Poe's "Diddling Considered as One of the Exact Sciences." Like Melville, Poe had already found the essence of the American in the con man:

> Poe states that "man was made to diddle" — that is, hoax, take advantage of, con. "This is his aim — his object — his end. And for this reason when a man's diddled we say he's '*done*.'" Poe defines diddling: "Minuteness, interest, perseverance, ingenuity, audacity, *nonchalance,* originality, impertinence, and *grin.*"

And what does Poe mean by "grin?"

> Grin: — Your *true* diddler winds up all with a grin. But this nobody sees but himself. He grins when his daily work is done — when his allotted

labors are accomplished—at night in his own closet, and altogether for his own private entertainment. He goes home. He locks his door. He divests himself of his clothes. He puts out his candle. He gets into bed. He places his head upon the pillow. All this done, and your diddler *grins.*[10]

Counter-Currents/*North American New Right,*
May 18, 2015

---

[10] J. Marshall Trieber, "A Study of Poesque Humor," from *Poe Studies,* December 1971, vol. IV, no. 2, 4: 32–34.

INDEX

'50s Nostalgia, 20n3

'60s, iii, 10, 11, 17, 27-30, 34, 37, 43, 49, 61, 67

A

A Dandy in Aspic, 49n9

"A Date with Your Family," 28n14

"A Gothic Love Song," vn4

Abrahams, Robin, 71n8

Absolutely Fabulous, 77n17

ACLU, 75

Acting White, 12n12

Adrian Leverkühn, 60n20

Advise and Consent, 34-38, 43-45, 53, 62- 64

Agent for H.A.R.M., 65n23

Al Cevic, 75n14

Alan Greenspan, 25-26

All in the Family, 31m18

All Quiet on the Western Front, 52n12

Alpha Male, 10, 24, 40, 79

Altars of the East, 52n12

Altars of the World, 52n12

AMC (cable network), 17, 34, 77

American Psycho, 64

Ames, Mark, 2

Anderson, Brig: see Anderson, Senator Brigham

Anderson, Senator Brigham (Brig), 35-39, 45-66

Animal House, 8, 75-76

Arab Spring, 33n23

Arab World, 33

Archie Bunker, 31n18

Arjuna, 55

The Art of Worldly Wisdom, 18

Aryan Civilization, iv

Aryan Man, 64, 79

Aryan Society, 10

Attack of the Giant Leeches, 11

Auschwitz, 69

Ayres, Lew, 35, 52n12

B
Bass, Saul, 34
Bastiat, Frédéric, 18
Batt, Bryan, 78n2
Beatnik, the, 32
Berman, Morris, 65n24
Berry, Wendell, 9n4
Better Call Saul, 77
Bhagavad Gita, 55n13
Biden, Joe, 46
bigamy, 40
blackmail, 34-38, 45, 62, 65
Blackshirts, 1
Blaze, The , 55n15
Bloom, Allan, 9
Bloomberg, Michael, 10
Blüher, Hans, 7
Bogart, Humphrey, 47n6
Bogdanovich, Peter, 34
Boggy Creek II: The Legend Continues, 16n22
Borgias, The, 20
Borgnine, Ernest, 9
Boston Globe, 71n8
Bowden, Jonathan, 41

Bratman, David, 36n25
Breaking Bad, 78
Breisacher, Dr. Chaim, 61n20
Breton, André, iiin2
Brie, Alison, 14-15
British Raj, 64n22
Bronx, The, 21, 82
Brooks, Mel, 26
Brown Shirts, 1
Buckley, William F., 11, 58
Buddha, 50
Buddhism, 52n12
Buffalo Bill, 40
Burckhardt, Jacob, 51, 66
Bush, George H. W., 2-3, 31
Bushwood Country Club, 75

C
Caddyshack, 68, 75, 81
Canaan, 55n14
Capone, Al, 50
Cardinal Spellman, 11
Carl the Grounds-keeper, 75n14, 76
Carnival of Souls, 75
Carson, Johnny, 26n11
Case, Arthur, epi-

graph
cash nexus, 21
casual Friday, 3
Catholics, 36; see al-
    so Irish Catholics
cavalier culture of
    the South, 65n24
Cayenne Pepper, 44,
    51
Center of the World,
    51, 57
Central America, 31
Chakravartin, 51, 57
Chambers, Whit-
    taker, 11
Cheever, John, 28n14
Christianity, 52
CIA, 27
cigarettes, 9n4
cigars, 9n5
circles, 77n16
civil rights, 37
Civil War, 30-31
The Civilization of the
    Renaissance in Ita-
    ly, 52n11
Coca-Cola, 79n3
Coen Brothers, 16,
    35, 77
Cohn, Roy, 11, 38
Cold War, 50n10
collegiality, 21, 33,
    39, 43-44
colors (gang cloth-
    ing), 2

Columbus and Rice,
    80
Commerce Secretary
    Bailey, 82
concentration
    camps, 33
Connelly, Edmund,
    19n2
conscientious objec-
    tion, 52n12
Cooley, Senator Sea-
    bright ("Seab"),
    34-35, 38-39, 47,
    51, 62, 66
Coomaraswamy, A.
    K., 60n20
Cooper, Bertram
    (Bert), 24-25, 37-
    39, 53-54, 60, 65,
    70-71, 74-76
Coppola, Francis
    Ford, 82
Cornwallis (British
    General), 58n16
Cosgrove, Ken, 70-
    71, 74, 75n14
cosmic cycles, 50
Costanza, George,
    28n14
Costello, Jef, 48n7
Counter-Currents,
    iii, v, 29n16, 18,
Craig, Carl, 14
Crawford, Joan,
    52n12

Crespino, Joseph, 38n28

crypsis, 68, 79n4, 82

CSA: The Confederate States of America, 30, 32

Cuddihy, John Murray, ivn3, 27n13, 69n4, 81n7

cynicism, 22, 33, 43-44

D

Da Fonz, see Fonzie

Dali, Salvatore, iiin2, 44

Dallas, Texas, 50n10

Dangerfield, Rodney (Jacob Cohen), 75n14

Daniel "D" Day, 77

Daniélou, Andre, 64n22

Das Rheingold, 57n16

De Blasio, Bill, 9

De Niro, Robert, 50, 82-83

Dean Wormer, 8, 75

Delta House, 76

Departed, The, 44n2

desegregation, 37

desertion, 40, 69

Dewey Ballantine, 21n5

diddling, 78-84

"Diddling Considered as One of the Exact Sciences." 83-4

Die Hard with a Vengeance, 19

Die Walküre, 59

Dignam, Staff Sgt., 44n2

DiNunno, Gina, 15n16

Dionysian indiscernibility, 2

Doctor Faustus. The Life of the German composer Adrian Leverkühn, told by a friend, 60n20

Donovan, Jack, 9, 46, 57

doubling, 44-45

Dr. Strangelove, or How I Stopped Worrying and Learned to Love the Bomb, 56

Draper, Betty, epigraph, 72, 79n2

Draper, Don, 6, 8, 10-11, 24-25, 35, 37, 39-40, 49, 53-54, 62-64, 69, 72-73, 75-77, 78-83

Drescher, Fran, 58n17

Drury, Allan, 34,

36n24, 38n27
Dylan, Bob, 33, 76

E
Eames chairs, 5
East Village, 79n5
Egypt, 55n15
Eldritch Evola & Others: Traditionalist Meditations on Literature, Art, & Culture, The, 28n15
Electric Kool-Aid Acid Test, The, 4
Emily Dickinson College, 76n14
"Entrance into Valhalla," 58n16
Epstein, Brian, 3
Esalen, 78, 80
"Essay on Liberation," 61n20
Esther, 55
European Right, 66n24
Europeans, 67
Evola, Baron Julius, 1-2, 6-7, 27n12, 49, 62
Eye of Horus, 59n18
Eye of Mordor, 70

F
Faber College, 76

Facebook, v
Fawkes, Guy, 60
FDR, 50n9
Federal Reserve, 22n6
Feminazis, 9
Field of Duty, 55n13
Fielding, Joseph, 60n19
Fire Island, 28n14
Firesign Theatre, 24
Fonda, Henry, 34, 48
Fonzie, 20n3, 28n14
Four Freshmen, 65n23
Francis, Coleman, 16n21
Frankfurt School, 11, 26-28, 81n7
Free Speech Zones, 2
Freud, Sigmund, 7, 10n6, 27, 81
Friedan, Betty, 15, 74
Fruit of Islam, 13n14

G
Gabriel Over the White House, 48n7
game, 17n23
Gandolfini, James, 6
Garbo, Greta, 47n5
gay bars, 35, 41, 65
gefilte fish, 74n12
General Jack Ripper, 56

genocide, 55
Germany, 1, 48, 61
Gettysburg, 30
Ginsberg, Michael,
    11, 69
Godfather II, 83
Goodfellas, 6
Goodman, Saul, 78
Google, 17
Gracián, Baltasar, 18
Greaney, Dan, 41n30
*Green Nazis in Space:
    New Essays on Lit-
    erature, Art, &
    Culture*, v
Greif, Mark, 4-6
Grizzard, George, 34
Groundhog Day,
    75n13
Guardian Angels, 2
Guénon, René, 50

H
Halson, Nick, 47n5
Haman, 53-57, 74n12
Hamm, Jon, 6, 16-17
Happy Days, 20-22
Harley, see Hudson,
    Vice President
    Harley
Harris, Jared, 56
Harris, Joan, 19, 43-
    47, 56, 60, 64-65,
    74, 79-80
Hein, Jon, 21

Henderson, William,
    21
Hendricks, Christi-
    na, 17
Hillcrest Country
    Club, 68
hippies, 2, 79-80
Hitler, Adolf. 29, 63
Hobart, Jim, 70
Hoffman II, Michael
    A., 19n2
*The Homo and the Ne-
    gro: Masculinist
    Meditations on Pol-
    itics and Popular
    Culture, The*, iiin1,
    33n23, 36n25,
    45n3, 46n5, 47n6
homophobia, 17, 33,
    38, 63n21
homosexuality, 6,
    33n23. 38n27
Hoover, Herbert, 31,
    76n14
*How Can You Be in
    Two Places At
    Once When You're
    Not Anywhere At
    All*, 24n8
*How to Succeed In
    Business without
    Really Trying*, 37
Howard Beale, iv
Hudson, Vice Presi-
    dent Harley, 35,
    45-60, 67

Human Potential
  Movement, 81
Hunt, Senator
  Lester, 38n27
Hyannis Port, 3

I
I'm All Right, Jack, 8
IBM typewriters, 5
Iliad, The, 41
Illinois Nazis, 2
Illuminati, 60n18
*IMDB (Internet Movie
  Database),* 34
In My Own Way, 81
Indiana University,
  21
Inglourious Basterds,
  29
iPhones, 32
Irish Catholics, 71-74
Israel, 32

J
J. Crew, 65n23
Jaguar (car), 34, 59
Jeremy Irons, 19
Jersey Shore, 41
Jesus, 82
Jews, 27, 61-62, 69,
  73-74, 77; see also
  Judaics
JFK Assassination, iv
JFK Look, 3, 36
Johnson, Dr. Grego-

ry, iiin1, v, 41n31
Judaics, 18, 20, 29-31,
  40, 60n20, 62, 60;
  see also Jews
Judge Smails, 68, 75
Jumping the Shark,
  20-22, 29-31, 44
Jung, Carl Gustav,
  10n6

K
Kartheiser, Vincent,
  16
*Keeping Up With the
  Steins,* 20n3
Kempton, Murray,
  70n6
Kennedy, Joe, 3
Kennedy, Sen. Ed-
  ward, 39
Kerouac, Jack, 76, 78
Knight, Ted, 36n24
Kraftwerk. 14
Kurtagic, Alex,
  32m21

L
Lattman, Peter, 21n5
Laughton, Charles,
  34
Lawford, Peter,
  36n24, 63

Lear, Norman, 31n18
LeBoeuf Lamb, 21n5

Lechter, Hannibal, 29

Lee, Spike, 30

Leffingwell, Robert, 34-37, 39, 45, 48, 51

Leftism, iii, 37, 38n28, 55n15, 65n24, 80

Leibowitz, Fawn, (RIP), 76n14

Leone, Sergio, 81-83

London (UK), 3, 8, 54

Los Angeles, 71

Los Angeles Country Club, 68

Lott, Trent, 38

Lucky Strike (brand), 40n29

Lukacs, John, 67

M

MacDonald, Kevin, 19n2, 31n18, 81n7

Madison Ave., 43, 71

Mallon, Thomas, 38n27

Malloy, Mike, 55n15

Malone, 56-57

Manhunter, 29, 75n13

Mann, Thomas, 61n20

Männerbund, iii, 1-7, 18, 21, 36n24,

46n5, 64n22

Man-o-sphere, 1, 12, 14

Manslaughter, 40, 69

Manson, Charles, 80n5

Manspreading, 1-7

Marcuse, Herbert, 27, 60n20

Margin Call, 19

Marlowe, Derek, 49n9

Marranos, 28n14

Marshall, Gary, 20n3

Marx, Karl, 21, 27

McCain, John, 63

McCann Erikson, 70-79

McCarthy, Sen. Joseph, 37

McGill, Bruce, 77

McGill, Jimmy, 77

Men Among the Ruins: Post-War Reflections of a Radical Traditionalist, 1

Men of Honor, 60

Menken, Rachel, 73, 76

Milgram Experiment, 29

Militarism, 33

Milwaukee, 20n3

Mind Control, 32

Minnesota, 16

Moby Dick, 66n24
Monty Python, 43
Mordecai, 55
Morse, Robert, 37, 62
Mosely, Sir Oswald,
   1
Murray, Bill, 76, 14
Murray, Don,
   35, 37
Museum of Jewish
   Heritage, 16n19
Muslims, 32
Mystery Science Thea-
   ter 3000 (MST3k),
   11n8, 16n22, 27m
   28n14, 34, 37n26
Myth of Punch, The,
   42, 60n19

N
Nanny, The, 58n17
Napoleon, 81n7
National Socialists
   ("Nazis"), v, 1-3,
   28-29
Ness, Elliot, 56
New Delhi, 54
New York City
   Subway, 9-11, 32-
   33
New York City, 2,
   32, 41
New York Daily
   News, 17
New York Times, 21,

   38n27
Newquist, Roy,
   52n12
Nietzsche, Friedrich,
   52
Ninth Symphony
   (Beethoven), 60
Nixon, Richard, v,
   24, 70n6
Noodles (character
   in *Once Upon a*
   Time in America),
   82
North, the, 30-31
NRA (National Rifle
   Association), 10

O
Obamacare, 31
Occidental Observer,
   The, 19
Of Two Minds, 22n6
Old Testament, 55
Once Upon a Time in
   America, 81-83
Onion AV Club, 72n9,
   72n9n, 72 n11
Oppression, 32
Ordeal of Civility, iv,
   27, 28n14,
The Ordeal of Civility:
   Freud, Marx, Levi-
   Strauss, and the
   Jewish Struggle
   With Modernity,
   iv3, 27n13, 69n4

Outgrowing Democracy: A History of the United States in the Twentieth Century, 67n26

P
Palin, Sarah, 26n11
Paranoiac-critical method, iii-iv, 44
Passing the buck, 50n9
Passing the Buck: A Traditionalist Goes to the Movies, v
Passover, 55n15
PC, 39
Peggy Olson, 75-77, 81
Pelfley, Leland ("Lee"), 9n4
Pequod, 65n24
Pete Campbell, 6-10, 16, 24, 37, 45, 58, 64, 74
Peter Paul and Mary, 61n20
Pidgeon, Walter, 34
Pleasantville, 32m21
Podhoretz, Norman, 31
Poe, Edgar Allen, 83-84
Point of Terror, 75n13
Pope Alexander, 19-20
Preminger, Otto, 35-36, 60, 65n23
President, The (unnamed, in Preminger film *Advise and Consent*), 35, 45-51
progressives, 61, 66
progress, v
propaganda, iv, 22
Pryce, Lane, 45, 47, 53-54, 59-62, 74n12, 81n8
Psycho (Hitchcock film), 36n24
Punch (character), 42, 61n19
Purdue, Tito, 9n4
Purim, 55, 60, 74
Puritanism, 9n6, 66n24
Purple Decades, The, 13m13

Q
Quakers, 65n24

R
racism, 32, 33
Radical Chic & Mau-Mauing the Flak Catchers, 13n13
Radziwell, Lee, 3
Rand, Ayn, 9, 25, 28,

36, 25
Randism, 25
Reagan, Ronald, 22
Red Zone Cuba,
16n21, 34, 37n29,
65
Reuben (character),
9n4
Reuben, 9n4
Revelation of the
Method, 18
Roger, Bunny, 47n6
Rolling Stone, 72n10
Roman Empire, 23
Romano, Salvatore,
78n2
Rome, 49
Runes, 56, 59-60
Runt, 46, 57-8, 74
Ryder, Charles, 20

S
Sailer, Steve, 68, 71,
79n4
satori, 79, 82
Schoenberg, Arnold,
60n20
Schopenhauer, Ar-
thur, 32
SCP West, 70n7
Seab, see Senator
Seabright Cooley
Second Vermont
Republic, 65n24
Secret Service, 37m

45-46, 58n16
*Secret Societies and
Psychological War-
fare,* 19n2
Seinfeld, 28n14
Sellers, Peter, 1
Senate Majority
Leader Robert
Munson, 36-38,
47, 62-63, 66
Senate, 34-39, 45-48,
51-52, 57-58, 64,
66
Sexism, 32, 33
Sgt. Pepper, 2, 10
shenanigans, 24
Siegel, Lee, 19n2
Siegfried, 59
Siegfried, 59
Simpsons, The, 41n30
Sinatra, Frank, 41
Slattery, John, 11n9
Slavery, 32
Slobs, 4, 8, 76
Smith, Charles
Hugh, 22n6
snobs, 8, 75, 81n7
Soprano, Tony, 6
Sopranos, The, 5-6,
78
South Carolina, 47
South, the, 30-31,
65n24
spiral, v, 46
SS, 1

St. Paul (city), 76
Starling, Clarice, 40
Stenbock, Count Eric, 42, 60n19
Sterling, Roger, 11, 54, 62, 65, 69, 73-77, 80-81
Sterling Cooper *et alia*, 19, 54, 63-64, 70-71, 74, 76, 79n3
Strom Thurmond's America, 38n28
Superior Man, 50, 57
Susan Ross, 28n14

T
TCA Awards, 11n9
Tea Party, 26n11
Teabaggers, 55n15
Teddy Boys, 3
Tentacle porn, 76
The Gap, 2
The New World, 65n24
Those Who Can See, 43
Thurmond, Sen. Strom, 37
Tibet, David, vn4
Tikkun olam, 26
Tom Jones, 61n19
Tone, Franchot, 34, 48n7
Touch of Evil, 78n1
Tradition, Family,

Property (right wing movement), 9n5
Traditionalism, 33n23
treason, 40
Trieber, J. Marshall, 84n10
Truman, Harry, 49n9

U
U.S., 22
U.S.S.R., 22
Übermensch, 9n4
Uncle Toms, 12n12
uniforms, 1-3
University of American Samoa Correspondence School of Law, 77
Urban Dictionary, 20n2, 26n11
Untouchables, The, (De Palma film), 36n25, 45-50

V
Van Ackerman, Senator Fred, 34-39, 45-50, 58, 62, 65
Van Patten, David, 64
Vermont, 65n24, 74
Victorian England, 23

Vidal, Gore, 31n18, 58
Vigilant Citizen (website), 16n18
Vega, Vince, 15n17, 20

W

Wall Street Journal, 19n2
Wall Street, 73
Wallace, 46, 57
War of the Roses, 31
Warhol, Andy, 63n21
WASPs, 10, 19, 24-28, 33, 41-44, 56, 60, 62, 65n24, 68-71, 73-75, 82-83
Watts, Alan, 80-81
Waxman, Henry, 25
Way of Men, The, 46n4
Weiner, Matthew, 5, 15-16, 24, 68, 71, 73, 78-83
Weininger, Otto, 7
Weiss, Phillip, 31n18
White trash, 14
White, Betty, 36n24

Why America Failed: The Roots of Imperial Decline, 65n24
Wikipedia, iv, 13n13, 20n3, 21n4, 78n18
Will Graham, 75n13
Winkler, Henry, 20n3
Wolfe, Tom, 4, 12-13
Woods, James, 82
Woodstock (music festival), 2
"The World in Flames," 32n20
World Tree, 57, 59
"The World Turn'd Upside Down, 58n16
Wotan, 56-60, 74
Wotan, 56-60, 75n12
Wyoming 34, 38n27
X, Malcolm, 13n14

Y

Yockey, Francis Parker, 32

Z

ZeroHedge, 22

ABOUT THE AUTHOR

James J. O'Meara was born in Detroit, educated in Canada, and now lives in an abandoned glove factory in America's Rust Belt. From atop this crumbling remnant of America's industrial might, he broods with morose delectation over the inevitable reappearance of the hordes of White youth known to history as the *Männerbünde*, or Wild Boys. His periodic bulletins on their activities appear on his blog, Where the Wild Boys Are at http://jamesjomeara.blogspot.com/.

He is the author of *The Homo and the Negro: Masculinist Meditations on Politics and Popular Culture*, ed. Greg Johnson (San Francisco: Counter-Currents, 2012), *A Review of James Neill's "The Origins and Role of Same-Sex Relations in Human Societies"* (Amazon.com: Kindle Editions, 2013), and *The Eldritch Evola . . . & Others: Traditionalist Meditations on Literature, Art, & Culture* (San Francisco: Counter-Currents, 2014). His articles and reviews have also been published by Counter-Currents/*North American New Right*, *Alexandria*, *FringeWare Review*, *Aristokratia*, and *Judaic Book News*.

www.ingramcontent.com/pod-product-compliance
Lightning Source LLC
Chambersburg PA
CBHW051817040426

42446CB00007B/714